Say It, See It, Be It

Say It, See It, Be It

How Visions & Affirmations
Will Change Your Life

Arlene Rosenberg

BookMarketingSolutions,LLC
The Publisher of Experts

Traverse City, Michigan

Say It, See It, Be It
How Visions & Affirmations
Will Change Your Life

by Arlene Rosenberg

Copyright © 2006 by Arlene Rosenberg

Published by:

BookMarketingSolutions,LLC
The Publisher of Experts

10300 E. Leelanau Court
Traverse City, Michigan 49684
orders@BookMarketingSolutions.com
www.BookMarketingSolutions.com

Printed in the United States of America

Rosenberg, Arlene.

Say it, see it, be it : how visions & affirmations will change your life / Arlene Rosenberg. — Traverse City, Mich. : BookMarketingSolutions, 2006.

p. ; cm.

ISBN-13: 978-0-9741345-7-4
ISBN-10: 0-9741345-7-0

1. Self-actualization (Psychology) 2. Affirmations. 3. Self-talk. 4. Imagery (Psychology) 5. Success. 6. Self-realization. 7. Self help techniques. I. Title.

BF637.S4 R67 2006
158.1—dc22

0601

This book is available at:
ReadingUp.com

Dedication

I dedicate this book to the angel here on earth who helped me discover my inner beauty, genius, and strength and taught me that I am never alone — Esther Creek.

Author's Note

Many names and identifying details of the client examples described in this book have been changed to preserve the confidentiality of the coaching relationship.

Contents

Acknowledgements *xi*

Introduction *1*
The Gift Of Tenacity

Part I

Chapter One *21*
Change Occurs From The Inside Out
1. Taking Ownership of the Results We Create *23*
2. Your Present Thoughts Determine Your Future *27*
3. You Have the Ability to Change Your Thoughts *28*
4. The Connection Between Self-Talk, Self-Image, and Affirmations *31*
5. Our Self-Talk Builds Our Self-Image *34*

Chapter Two *39*
Fear: An Extension Of The Ego Thought System
1. Fear Forms in the Subconscious *39*
2. Understanding the Effects of Fear *41*
3. The Myth of Security *42*
4. Fear Is Learned in Childhood *43*

Chapter Three *45*
Negative Thinking Is Passed Unconsciously
From Generation To Generation
1. Criticism of Others Is an Extension of Our Self-Loathing *47*
2. Letting Go of the Need to Be Perfect *49*
3. Procrastination Is Just Another Form of Fear *55*
4. Creating Self-Esteem – Learn How to Set Boundaries *56*

Chapter Four *59*
Symptoms And Outcomes Of Negative Thinking
1. The Symptoms *59*
2. Victim Thinking Stunts Our Personal Development *65*
3. "To Compare Is to Despair" *67*
4. Hypersensitivity to Mistakes *68*
5. Always Seeking Validation *70*
6. The Value of Finding a Mentor or Coach *72*
7. The "What If?" Trap *74*
8. The Burden of Overresponsibility *75*
9. Missing the Present to Live in the Past or the Future *77*

Chapter Five 79
Symptoms And Outcomes Of Living Freely
1. The Symptoms of Living Freely 79
2. Making Time for Journaling 82

Part II

Chapter One 87
Taking Command Of Your Life
1. Actual Experience versus Imagined Experience 87
2. Letting Go of the Old Precedes All Change 89
3. Visualization Is a Tool That Can Help Us 91
   Reprogram Our Thinking
4. The Leading Achiever Development Wheel 92
5. Skirting the Fear Trap 94
6. Setting the Stage to Create Visions That Work 94
7. Using the Leading Achievers Development Wheel 96
8. You've Got to Be Kidding! 113

Chapter Two 117
The Power Of Affirmations
1. How Affirmations Work 117
2. The Art of Detachment 118
3. Uses for Affirmations 119
4. Develop Your Own Affirmations 120
5. Creating Effective Affirmations 124
6. Steps for Maximizing the Effectiveness of Your Affirmations 128
7. Relaxation Exercise 129
8. Sample Affirmations 130

Conclusion *139*

Bibliography *143*

About the Author *145*

Acknowledgement

There have been so many people who supported me with unconditional love and understanding on my incredible journey that I cannot publish this book without thanking the following:

- First, my Higher Power, who guides me in every endeavor and never lets me down.

- My husband, George, who is my biggest earthly supporter and has stood by me through the many faces and changes of Arlene.

- Wendy Steinbaum and Joan Haberman, who have taught me the meaning of unconditional friendship.

- My sisters in the *Circle of Light*, who have shown me how a healthy family functions.

- To every one of my clients who have been my teachers.

• The people who made this book possible: Bill Greaves, a great
  artist and friend; Steve Tyra, a mentor who suggested the book
  title; Laura Orsini, for helping me get the project started, motivating me and editing the first draft; Thomas White my publisher; and Ilene Stankiewicz, who made the final edits.

• Alison Lenox, who keeps me organized no matter how much
  trouble I get into.

How Visions & Affirmations
Will Change Your Life

Introduction
The Gift of Tenacity

For more than 15 years, I have been on an incredible internal journey of changing the way I think and feel about myself. I was raised in a home environment where I never felt safe or secure because of unrelenting psychological and physical abuse. As I grew up, it became more and more difficult to trust myself and the world around me. My internal journey has involved emancipation from crippling fear and insecurity, and a move toward the discovery of the person I really am — as opposed to the person I was always expected to be. My continual search for new levels of fulfillment and self-empowerment — in both my business and personal life — finally seems to be paying off. This opening has helped me find my true sense of self and my life's purpose, and has taught me that I am not a puppet of those around me. My thoughts, feelings, and beliefs are valuable and crucial to my existence — and to my success. I now understand that no one has the right to control my thinking or my body.

Today, in every situation, I know I always have the ability to make a choice about the best decisions for myself and my life. By reprogramming my old belief system and using the tools described in this book, I learned to think positively "of myself" and "for myself," and I stopped second-guessing everything I attempted to do. I have developed new habits, attitudes, and beliefs that consistently promote my well-being. A new self-reliance has allowed me to look at others positively and interact with them in ways that work for them and for me. This emancipation process has left me with a sense of freedom about my power to direct my own life. I have discarded an old way of thinking that included living with mild depression daily and viewing my world through fearful, negative eyes. Now I see myself as a creator, someone who lives in the realm of unlimited possibility. I see each moment as a new opportunity to achieve more in my life.

Moreover, I learned that as soon as I began to love and accept myself, people wanted to be with me. Strangely enough, that made it easier for me to see the good in them, and accept them unconditionally. Fewer and fewer negative, unhappy people began to appear in my life, and if they did show up, they quickly disappeared. My need to worry about what others thought of me began to fade away, and I learned to become choosy about whom I spend my time with.

But this growth did not occur overnight. It took many years of work to go from a non-functioning, battered child to a self-reliant individual, and even now there are times when self-doubt tries to rear its ugly head. But I am strong enough to counterbalance the old self-sabotaging beliefs when they try to sneak through; I can catch them and immediately replace them with positive beliefs and affirmations that do serve me.

My gift of tenacity kept me on an endless search to find the love and recognition I had never experienced during my childhood, and has sustained me through every step of changing and reprogramming myself. Something very deep within me has driven me to never give up on this search. I believe that the perfection expected from me as a child was behind my quest, but was only one motivating factor. Something more universal was pushing me to heal myself, and today I trust that it was my higher self.

The month I learned to ride a two-wheeler best illustrates my persistence. At the age of seven, my best friend contracted polio. This was in the 1950s, before Jonas Salk discovered a vaccine to prevent this deadly disease from striking young children and adults. Out of necessity, I was quarantined in my home for six weeks. By the end of the fourth week, my parents allowed me to go outside and ride my bike up and down our short street. I am sure by that point everyone must have needed a break from the stress and pressure of my confinement and the energy of keeping a healthy seven-year-old quiet.

Within two days of endlessly riding up and down the street, I asked my father to remove my training wheels from my new Schwinn two-wheeler. Unbelievably, on the third day after he came home from work, he removed them. After practicing with me twice, he told me I was ready, and left me on my own to ride and balance the bike. All I did for the next week was ride up and down the street, wobbling and frequently falling over, scratching the fenders of the bike, my elbows, and my knees. Nothing was going to stop me, including the reprimands and criticisms I would get from my mother about damaging my new bike. It was almost as if I were possessed. And of course, by the beginning of my last week at home, I was no longer falling off or losing my balance: I had learned to ride my new two-wheeler like the big kids.

I am so grateful that I did not contract the disease, and that my friend survived with no severe aftereffects. However, the true significance of this story is that I learned about a deep force within me that helped me succeed. As the years went on and I suffered emotionally, I lost connection with this force at times. Yet there were moments when it resurfaced, giving me the courage to walk through my fears, take risks, and keep searching.

I now realize that my parents were unable to give me the love I needed because they were unable to love themselves. From my new vantage point, it is obvious that they desperately needed love, but they had no clue how to receive it from or give it to others. They wanted me to be what they were not, and I could not live up to their standards, no matter how hard I tried. This was the most disconcerting realization, one that led to my feelings of never being enough or doing enough. Eventually I became aware that no matter how hard I worked to gain their love, I would never do it correctly in their eyes because they were so unhappy with their own existence. They were trying to mentally and physically beat out of me the very things they hated about themselves.

Incredibly, my path to this monumental shift opened up for me when I made a major life move from New York to Atlanta in 1986. Until that time, nothing I tried seemed to work for very long. Therapy didn't seem to be the answer; while motivational seminars and self-help books were briefly inspiring, within a few days of attending or reading them, I fell back into the same emotional space I had started from.

My life changed forever when I met a life and spiritual coach by the name of Esther Creek. Esther's unconditional support and unconventional methods enabled me to gain a new outlook, a new vision, and a new purpose. It took two occasions of sitting next to her (no accident, of course) at a United Way committee meeting before we made a connection and she invited me to her home to learn more about her beliefs and teachings.

Esther's ideas were so foreign to me that I remember planning an escape route in my mind: If I discovered she was too nutty, I would swiftly leave her house before she could harm me mentally. However, I quickly learned that this was no crazy person. And although I didn't immediately comprehend everything Esther was sharing with me, she was probably the first individual who understood me and the frustration I felt about my life. Almost immediately Esther pointed out how negative my words and thoughts were. This observation caught me by total surprise, as I was completely unaware that I had been poisoning my own mind for so long with the things I continually said to myself through a process known as negative self-talk. Esther had the knowledge and answers to teach me about the changes I needed to make that would allow me to unleash my full potential. I was clear about one thing: I wanted everything she had to offer.

Although my old belief systems at first made me skeptical that I could be successful, I began to succeed despite myself. Esther introduced me to the *Law of Attraction* and explained how it expanded negativity in my life. Simply stated, the law says, "We gravitate toward and become like that which we think about, regardless of whether it is beneficial for us or not." The science of quantum mechanics and physics validates the truth of this law, and will be discussed later in this book.

Esther described how both my thoughts and spoken words created internal laws that were keeping me unsuccessful and unfulfilled. She taught me to observe my "mind chatter," and I began to hear how frequently I said things to myself like, "If only I had done this or that, then I would truly have succeeded." It was rare, if ever, that I congratulated myself on a job well done. All I could see was the continued failure, so I didn't know how to appreciate my accomplishments. My negativity prevented me from seeing what was good. Esther helped me realize I was always looking for four-leaf clovers to wish upon. I did not understand that with my subconscious mind, my own spoken words and beliefs would bring me the "good luck" I was continually searching for.

Staying stuck in my problems and negative mind chatter blocked me from hearing my true inner voice or intelligence. With Esther's guidance, I quickly comprehended that we all have a real choice. We can live in the solution rather than in the problem, and we can substitute positive thoughts and attitudes for negative ones. I began to understand that staying positive would propel me into action, while remaining negative and victimized would pull me into a downward spiral of inaction and feelings of unworthiness and unfulfillment.

At the same time that I was working with Esther, I started reading every book I could get my hands on that dealt with positive thinking, success, and reaching one's full potential. In one such book, *Power vs. Force*, author David Hawkins shares information gleaned through his nearly 30 years of research regarding the energy levels of individual and large-group consciousness. Hawkins reveals that 87 percent of humanity is functioning at extremely weak energy levels, or low levels of consciousness. What this means, in essence, is that the majority of people in our world are functioning at extremely low levels of awareness and motivation. This translates into a world population where anger, guilt, hatred, judgment, blame, conflict, manipulation, conditional forgiveness, fault-finding, and scarcity run rampant. Isn't it sad that the majority of the human race is unable to see and recognize the incredible power they have within them to manifest all the happiness and joy they so desperately desire?

Hawkins's book, as well as many others, confirms that for hundreds of years philosophers and scientists like Socrates, Emerson, and Einstein have been teaching that human thoughts create everything we have — or do not have — in our lives. Through the combination of Esther's guidance and my own personal studies, I began to realize that it was entirely possible to change my thoughts, habits, and attitudes, and that the choice was totally up to me. However, this option meant I would need to release the set of self-imposed rules and limitations I had been carrying around with me since early childhood.

Looking back now, I realize that it didn't take long for the new feelings of freedom, hope, and empowerment to emerge. Exciting new things started to happen. My confidence began to grow and I started to trust myself in ways I had never believed were possible. I took the risk of starting a new career, making new friendships, and creating a totally different relationship with my family. The whole process was incredible. An entirely new life started to materialize for me. For one thing, I became less ego-driven, and developed much greater patience and tolerance toward others. My jealousies, anger, and resentment began to melt away.

As I became less self-absorbed, I was able to easily recognize the lower-energy people Hawkins described. For the first time, I could clearly see that many of the individuals in the world around me were experiencing pain and suffering. A large number of the people I was meeting had lost their way and were struggling with issues similar to mine. Just as I had been, they seemed unaware of their pessimism and how it dominated — and undermined — their lives. Newly equipped to notice these behaviors, I could instantly see how their negative attitudes were manifested in the way they treated themselves and others. I now understood that the roots of their malaise lay in their belief systems.

Many of my friends and colleagues had forgotten how to naturally be happy and enjoy life. They did not understand that as they looked for happiness and fulfillment outside of themselves, they had set up a habit of dependency that continually fed their negativity. Maybe their childhoods were less traumatic than mine, maybe they were more traumatic. Regardless of the specifics of their history though, everyone seemed to be carrying scars that prevented them from succeeding at their highest level.

As I began to share my success story and my new tools for living with those around me, I received responses that helped me understand how starved people were for this information. At about the same time, I attended a course for entrepreneurs. The instructor presented the traditional blaming, defensive perspective that I was just learning to overcome. Incredibly, I began to attract members of the class away from the instructor's negative viewpoint to my new way of thinking. These people ultimately formed my first coaching group.

The more I learned and grew and became comfortable with the language of positive thought, the more people began asking me if I could help move them toward their own personal fulfillment and the achievement of their goals. There was no doubt in my mind about helping them — the answer was YES! It was clear — my destiny was tied to teaching others a way of self-empowerment that could not fail. I wanted to share with them the "gift" I had been given. This book is my attempt to offer thanksgiving for the wonderful gift I received — the gift of myself — by helping others to learn to love themselves and those around them.

I recognized that I could help the people I was working with become successful by motivating them to raise their consciousness and teaching them how to be self-reliant, rather than remaining dependent on the thinking of others. I knew that to become a positive thinker and self-empowered human being, it was necessary to let go of every ounce of self-disapproval. The key to my own success had been my ability to replace my mindset of self-loathing with one of acceptance and self-love.

Until this point, I had seen myself as uncertain, fearful, and unable to comprehend the purpose of my life. I always felt I was an outsider, thinking, "Everybody else is so happy, why can't I be?" I could never see my own goodness, or acknowledge my strengths and accomplishments; it was very easy to pick myself apart and see only my weaknesses. I continually second-guessed myself, never feeling quite confident about any of my decisions. I never really knew I could give myself permission to live my life in the way *I* wanted to. In my belief that I was not enough, I created a wall of self-protection. The thought of exerting my views, needs, and desires over those of my parents, friends, teachers, and spouse scared me silly — it was, literally, beyond my comprehension.

Because of the many unpleasant things that occurred during my childhood, I had lost my faith. I viewed my Higher Power as a punisher like my parents, not as one who loved me unconditionally. I was completely unable to get in touch with my higher self. The greatest gift of this journey has been my ability to form a relationship with my Higher Power. I recognize that not only is the strength of the Universe around me, but inside me as well. When I let go and align with this power, I can create miracles for myself which not only benefit me, but all those around me. The "kingdom of heaven" is in each one of us — to access it, we need only allow ourselves to view our lives from a different perspective. As long as we are open to changing our present belief systems, we all have the power to stop creating the "hell" in which we live, no matter what kind of terrible things have happened to us in the past.

I have learned to stop worrying, and I release my fear because of this new relationship I have created. I no longer feel alone. Learning to release fear and "let go" has been the most difficult part of my journey. My journey has also led me to become a kinder, more tolerant, and humbler individual, one who can love someone even when I don't like their behavior. I have stopped blaming others and now have the ability to look at myself and own the part I play in the events of my life. I have learned to be self-reliant. I see the internal beauty in myself and others. I understand that my purpose for being here is to simply help other people raise their consciousness to new levels. Today I realize I spent a great deal of my early life trying to please everyone around me at my own expense, and it made me totally miserable. I now recognize and acknowledge my intelligence, my sacredness, my beauty — and I also admit to my weaknesses, or warts, as I call them. I accept all of me.

Interestingly, ever since I learned to free myself from the shadow of those around me and began coaching people, I have had many clients thank me for giving them "permission" to take the actions that would meet their needs, rather than constantly giving in to the demands of their bosses, parents, children, and spouses. These situations have had happy endings because each client took a major step forward to reclaim their power and experience the pride one feels when taking care of himself or herself.

Just as I had seen the Law of Attraction work in my own life, I began to see it work for others as I successfully coached them around the same principle. And the more people I coached, the more I realized that the knowledge and ideas I was sharing needed to be reduced to a simple system that could easily be followed. The Leading Achievers Development System emerged naturally to help people through the process of changing their thinking and their lives. This book is dedicated to helping you, the reader, learn how to use the two most important elements of this system — visions and positive affirmations — to create a world of possibility, joy, and success. The only prerequisites are an outrageous hunger to develop the self-knowledge and self-awareness that will help you change your thinking and a willingness to implement and use the ideas and information presented in this book.

Recently, I took a six-week Bible study class and sat next to Delores, a quite personable, well-educated woman in her late 50s. As we began talking, she revealed how she had grown up never really feeling empowered and having very few dreams about what she could or would accomplish in her life. She admitted to having suffered from low self-esteem and a poor self-image since her childhood, and she felt this was a problem shared by many women, especially those of her generation. Delores said that after her children started school, she made the decision to obtain a law degree and then became a law professor.

When it was my turn to share with Delores the details of my life, and I told her I was writing this book and professionally speaking on the subject of empowerment, she indicated that my work seemed to her so much more meaningful and accomplished than her chosen profession. It was difficult for her to comprehend that we were both accomplished, just in different areas, with different skill sets. She had totally minimized the achievement of getting her law degree and passing the bar exam.

Dolores confided that she was presently up for a promotion, however such a jump would mean she would have to learn new things, and she was quite comfortable right where she was. She didn't want to take a chance on experiencing any career challenges during her last few years before retirement. Even though the promotion would mean more money and prestige, it would be easier for her to simply stay put. In truth, Delores's inability to move forward was about fear and the inability to step beyond her comfort zone.

Even more distressing though, were the great feelings of sadness Delores shared about her college-educated son who also was suffering from a lack of purpose and self-esteem. Apparently, her son was preparing to take a job that was completely beneath his education level or abilities. I gently explained that I believed our thinking is passed down from one generation to the next. Clearly Dolores's son was highly influenced by his mother's belief system, and those beliefs were now playing out in his inability to see himself in a good, high-paying job. Delores immediately acknowledged the accuracy of this suggestion, and agreed that this issue was directly related to personal empowerment. During the length of a single conversation, Dolores began opening up to new thinking and mentioned that she was going to help her son find a coach who could enable him to form new, empowered perspectives.

Do you see yourself in any of these stories? Mine? Delores's? Delores's son? If so, I urge you to set aside some time each day to do the exercises presented at the end of each chapter in this book, so you can develop the self-awareness and honesty required to make internal changes. Use a special notebook or journal dedicated just for this work. Jot down your thoughts and ideas as they develop — do not let your ego convince you to put it off. Anyone with a strong desire to reach higher levels of consciousness and achievement can move beyond their traditional modes of thinking and reach their unlimited potential if they are willing to work the processes described in this book. Take the time to discover the incredible gift you are, and release the negative masks and blocks that have been holding you back.

I have personally watched hundreds of clients use these methods to grow and become personally and professionally successful. Once you truly believe that you can create different results in your life by shifting your thinking, you will: learn to live in possibility; create clear, focused visions and positive affirmations; and continuously use the Law of Attraction. It is an unbeatable formula for success.

Early on, I was told that shifting my thinking would be the hardest work I had ever done, but also the most rewarding. Yes, there were many days I lost faith and wanted to give in to my ego and go back to the negative but comfortably familiar habits that had kept me stuck. But as my life began to change for the better, I knew I would never go back to those tired, old belief systems.

You might be wondering how my personal story relates to my success in business. The answer is, in every way. If you learn nothing else from this book, please know that you are not alone. I have been where you are — feeling like nothing you try will ever work out, knowing there is more waiting for you but having no idea how to get there, and wondering why you try and try and strive and strive just to wind up back in the same place where you began. But there is hope. The story I've lived has proven to me that my current situation is a direct result of what I am feeling, thinking, and believing. And the same is true for you. Change the way you think, and your entire life will change with you.

Right this minute you are using the Law of Attraction to attract everything you have — and everything you do not have — in your personal and professional life. The good news is that no matter what your life looks like today, you can change it and move forward. Good can and will come from what right this minute appears to be chaos and catastrophe.

I was blessed because I never gave up. I survived because I was willing to walk through the pain of changing my habits, attitudes, and belief systems. To this day, I continue searching for answers. I regularly put in the time to use the tools that helped me discover and better myself, and I always make them my top priority. These tools include journaling, meditating, attending lectures and seminars, 12-step programs, and more. As a result, I've learned that when I take time for myself first, I always come out ahead. This can be a challenging concept in today's world, and the thought of putting yourself first may seem selfish. But the fact is that if you don't take care of yourself first, you will have nothing to give to anyone else. I now constantly search for people who have succeeded in spite of great difficulty and are willing to allow me to learn from them. They have become my mentors and my support system.

One of the most important relationships in my life is my 38-year marriage to my husband. Given the 50 to 60 percent divorce rate today, that is no small feat. We have been together since I was 20 years old, and over these years I have learned to respect him and accept him for who he is, and who he isn't. Like all the other changes I have made in my life, this has taken a great deal of effort and energy, and has at times been very painful for both of us. When we met, neither of us had been exposed to a relationship where two people knew how to love each other interdependently, which means being supportive while allowing each other to grow. This made things between us very difficult for many years. Fortunately, that old tenacity kicked in again, and in this case neither one of us ever gave up. We keep working on our relationship daily, and although it's far from perfect, it gets better and stronger each day. In fact, we've probably grown more because of the some of the tough experiences we've shared.

Take, for example, the circumstances that brought us from New York City to our desert life in Scottsdale, Arizona. Five years ago, on a bitterly cold, sleety, late-winter morning in New York

City, my husband and I left our apartment building to do what most New Yorkers do . . . head for the gym. Halfway down the street, my husband stopped me and said, "We are out of here."

I stopped still in my tracks, wearing some three pairs of socks, clunky rubber boots, pantyhose, two layers of clothes, a vest, and a down parka with ear muffs and a nose cover that was a gift from an Eskimo friend. I looked at him and said, "You've got to be kidding."

"No," George said. "I'm quite serious. I've had it with New York and this weather."

"Can we at least keep walking toward the gym as we discuss this?" I asked.

He grunted, then continued speaking. "I'm talking about leaving New York and moving to Arizona to create a working retirement." Now he had my full attention, because this was a plan we had vaguely discussed some time ago.

My tone changed and I said, "Absolutely! I could be up for that . . . except, dear, we have one major problem. We don't really have enough money. You know your business is not doing very well because we seem to be heading into a recession."

George responded by saying, "You know better than that, Arlene. If we believe we can live and run our businesses in Arizona while having a better quality of life, it will happen. We don't have to know how, yet." And with that, he walked, and I waddled on to the gym.

We started thinking seriously and strategically about how we would manage the big move. However a few months later, the tragedy of September 11th occurred, and the outlook for the move became worse, not better. Although everyone in the country was affected, the attacks had a dramatic and serious effect on those of us living in New York.

For economic reasons, George and I decided to downsize and move from our beautiful, somewhat spacious, two-bedroom apartment into a teeny-tiny one-bedroom with barely enough room for me to use a snack table as my desk. We put much of our furniture into three large wooden crates in a storage facility, along with those special possessions like family pictures, George's bronzed first pair of shoes, and some very expensive pieces from better times.

We settled in as best as we could, but never truly gave up on our vision to move to Arizona to create a living retirement. Deep down, both George and I had come to believe this was all happening for a purpose, and some sort of correction was occurring in our lives. In fact, whenever I would succumb to fear or doubt, a like-minded friend or mentor would magically appear or call to boost my spirits.

After about three months in our new apartment, I came in from shopping one Saturday afternoon, lugging several shopping bags — a very New York City experience because almost no one in Manhattan drives a car — to be greeted by some surprising news. I was huffing and puffing when my husband said, "Arlene, put your things down and sit for a minute."

Immediately, I was on alert. "Oh, no. What's happened now?" I asked.

Looking straight at me, George said, "Well, we received a letter from the storage facility today . . . and they've had an arson fire. It appears that many of our possessions have been damaged or destroyed."

All I could say was, "You're joking," even as I knew he was dead serious.

Seeing my spirits start to fall, George said, "I wish I were, but I'm not."

Well, people have limits, and I have to admit that I got more than a little upset. I screamed, "I've had it! No more! I can't take it!!!"

The fire damage to our belongings was devastating news, especially after everything we'd already been through. However, within a very short period of time, we began to see the *gift* in this seemingly horrible event. We learned that our insurance covered full-market replacement value, which meant we would receive current value for everything we had lost. Once we began pricing our destroyed possessions, it quickly became apparent that we would have enough money to purchase a home in Arizona and pay for the move.

The Law of Attraction continued to appear as calls started coming in from financial advisors and real estate people in Arizona who helped us get approved for a mortgage when we doubted that we would. And many other details just smoothly fell into place. Our lives were definitely starting to move in a new direction.

Truthfully, I don't encourage you to attract a fire to manifest the changes you seek in your life, but I hope you're beginning to at least consider the possibility that the Universe does conspire to support you. What you focus on does come to fruition — but it's up to you to choose whether that focus is on positive results or negative ones.

Say It, See It, Be It! is a book of hope for the thousands of people who feel disempowered and are not experiencing a sense of joy and/or satisfaction from their work, relationships, or life in general. Unfortunately, this scenario seems to apply to the majority of people in today's society. If you allow it to, this book will begin to open you up to a new way of thinking based on choice and possibility, and it will give you tools and methods to help you with the transition. Throughout the book, you will encounter exercises that will require you to think about and explore your feelings, beliefs, and motivations. You will likely find some of these exercises challenging, but I encourage you to work through them anyway.

My suggestion is for you to read through the entire book first. Then commit 30 minutes every other day to going through the demanding exercises. In between, I suggest you journal about the thoughts and feelings that are surfacing. The ideas and exercises you will encounter will free you to raise your consciousness and uncover your sacredness, higher self, and inner beauty so that you will have no trouble creating and manifesting your heart's desires.

If you are frustrated with the lack of progress in your life, feel unworthy, and wonder what your true purpose is, dear reader, please turn the page and get started.

Part I

Chapter One
Change Occurs from the
Inside Out

Reaching one's potential is no longer an option for most of us. It is the key to successful survival in today's chaotic world. However, reaching one's full capability often requires tearing down an old mindset and replacing it with a new one. This process is not an easy task and requires a commitment to monumental change. Those who choose this route, who are willing to walk the up-and-down steps of this journey, will experience unbelievable rewards.

The first step on this pathway to our full potential is to take a personal inventory and pinpoint the specific things in our careers, relationships, and social and spiritual lives we find less than satisfying. We want to determine the areas where we're merely settling, rather than being completely satisfied.

The only way to begin to change this dissatisfaction is by changing ourselves from within, on the subconscious level. For thousands of years the great masters have told us that all change "comes from the inside and works its way outward." Sadly, most people have a difficult time comprehending that they themselves must change. They find it easier to look outward and blame others for their failures and mistakes. On the other hand, people who are ready to take responsibility for their behavior, attitudes, and habits find it easy to open the door to levels of success they previously believed impossible.

R$_x$ercise

What are your reasons for reading this book? What has brought you to the point of being ready to transcend your old way of thinking and create a new belief system? How do you know you are ready?

_____

_____

_____

_____

_____

_____

_____

_____

_____

_____

_____

_____

What support system(s) do you have in place to help you with the ups and downs of this journey? If you don't feel you have any support system(s), what would it take for you to create one?

_____

_____

_____

_____

_____

_____

_____

_____

_____

_____

_____

_____

1. Taking Ownership of the Results We Create

I once had a client named Chris, who was a senior executive at a Midwest insurance firm, and he was miserable. It seemed that no matter how he performed for his boss, he received only criticism for his end results. Interestingly, this apparently was not the first time Chris had found himself in this situation.

Chris hired me to do two things for him: (1) help him to keep from getting fired before he found another job; and (2) help him to get his bosses to treat him less critically.

The first thing I asked Chris to do was to examine his part in the present situation. Initially, Chris could not accept the fact that he had played any role whatsoever in the behavior he was being subjected to. It had never dawned on him that his own actions might be provoking the negative responses he was receiving from his boss.

I asked Chris to share some of his self-talk with me. When Chris described the language he used to talk to himself, it quickly became apparent that he had little regard for his own capabilities and was subconsciously setting himself up for the negative responses he was receiving from others.

Over a period of several months, Chris was able to take a closer look at his internal responses and self-criticism. He slowly began to substitute positive affirmations every time he caught himself in self-criticism, and he started using self-affirming praise when he found himself doing something well. Although he did wind up losing that particular job, Chris was able to land a new position several months later for a higher salary, working for an entirely different type of employer.

Chris's energy had changed, and in turn, it led him to a more positive work environment with people who respected each other. The last time we spoke, Chris told me he had been promoted to vice-president and had been placed on the employee development team.

R$_x$ercise

Jot down the times in the past week when you blamed others — at work and/or at home — and your reasons for blaming them. Did you examine your part in the event before or after you laid blame elsewhere? If not, what prevented you from accepting ownership for your part in what happened?

_____

_____

_____

_____

_____

_____

_____

_____

_____

_____

_____

_____

_____

_____

_____

_____

_____

_____

_____

_____

_____

_____

_____

_____

_____

_____

_____

If you had the opportunity to repeat some of these events, how might you handle things differently?

_____

_____

_____

_____

_____

_____

_____

_____

_____

_____

_____

_____

_____

_____

_____

_____

_____

_____

_____

_____

_____

_____

_____

2. Your Present Thoughts Determine Your Future

Every thought that crosses one's mind is responsible for what they presently have or do not have in their life. In *The Success Book*, John Randolph Price says, "It is *your* consciousness, and not the consciousness of others, that shapes your life and molds your world." Each word and thought we think is an affirmation — it reinforces a positive *or negative* belief.

When we consciously use positive affirmations, they work to change our subconscious pictures, and subsequently manifest our dreams, goals, and, if we desire, an entirely new reality. Likewise, if we constantly focus on negative thoughts or words, such as, "I can't afford this," or "This isn't good enough," we begin to create those sorts of pictures in our lives. Every thought and word we speak is an affirmation, which either works for or against our wishes and desires.

R$_x$ercise

Take a moment to reread the last sentence of the previous paragraph. Seriously consider the type of power we have as individuals. Write down your thoughts about this awesome power. Do you believe this statement? If so, how can you begin making it work for you in your life?

---

3. You Have the Ability to Change Your Thoughts

We all have unlimited potential within us. And when we learn how to use our thoughts properly, we can become extraordinarily powerful human beings. My own personal experiences using positive affirmations — and those of my clients — have taught me that everyone is capable of noticing their negative thoughts and replacing them with positive affirmations. The only thing that holds us back is ourselves. You have everything you need right now to create the life you have always imagined.

> *You have everything you need <u>right now</u>*
> *to create the life you have always imagined.*

It's possible that by now you may be quite skeptical as you read about these ideas. This is a completely understandable feeling. Remember how uncertain I was when I first met Esther? The entire process is a bit easier to accept when you realize that it's all very scientific. We're not talking about "woo-woo" ideas or some strange New Age philosophy, but about the very real science of energy.

Scientists studying the field of quantum physics have proven that all thoughts are a form of energy. In her book *Secrets of Attraction*, Sandra Anne Taylor explains that "everything — all of life, from the solid mass of the earth to every object and being on it — pulses with energetic frequencies." Since our thoughts are unconscious positive or negative affirmations, we are continuously sending out energy in the form of statements or commands to the Universe.

Taylor continues: "Therefore, although it may seem that only the person doing the affirmations is hearing the words, this is not the case. The energy of these words, repeatedly thought, spoken, or written, goes out to the Universe in waves. We immediately begin to attract and resonate with the energy of the people, places, or things we are thinking about. Therefore, we are transmitting and receiving from people, places, and things every moment of our lives." Price sums up this idea of attractive energy with his statement: "Everything comes to you or is repelled by you based on the vibration of your energy field, and the vibration is established by your beliefs and convictions."

Think of yourself as a radio. When you are tuned into one station, you cannot hear another. You can only be in sync with one frequency at a time. When the things you desire and your everyday thoughts are aligned, you are on the same vibrational wavelength. You know you are in tune because you feel good. You know when you are out of sync (not on the same wavelength) when you do not feel good.

Science continues to confirm for us that affirmations are a powerful tool for creating change in our lives, whether by way of physical alterations or by attracting new people, things, and situations. Affirmations are so powerful in fact, that they seem almost magical. However quantum physics has shown us there is nothing magical about them. By modifying our subconscious thought processes through the use of positive affirmations, corresponding meaningful and lasting changes in behavior have no choice but to follow.

There are three major stipulations for making affirmations work:

- *Believe and accept at a deep level that your desires will manifest themselves.*
- *Experience the emotion of receiving your desire.*
- *Allow the miracle to happen in its own way and time.*

Even though they eventually agree that affirmations can work, most people fail to realize that changing the negative programming they acquired over many years is not a quick-fix process. The development of an entirely new attitude and belief system takes constant work, as well as patience, faith, and time. It is a virtual certainty, though, that those who are able to stick to this path and walk through their fears will see their lives change.

R$_x$ercise

As human beings, we hold on to old belief systems because they continue to serve us. Sometimes it is easier to continue to remain stuck than it is to change, if only because the stuck place has become incredibly comfortable, even as it stifles the life you really want to live. With as much honesty as possible, journal for a bit about your fears of letting go and releasing your negative thought patterns. Why have you chosen to hold on to old beliefs about lack, limitations, feelings of failure, and scarcity? How has holding on to these beliefs continued to serve you — until now?

_____

_____

_____

_____

_____

_____

_____

_____

_____

_____

_____

4. The Connection Between Self-Talk, Self-Image, and Affirmations

It is vital that while we examine our old thought patterns and belief systems, we become aware of the importance of our self-talk. Self-talk is described as the endless flow of chatter in our minds that constantly interprets everything we think, say, and do. Self-talk is a continually playing litany of affirmations — negative or positive — and has a very strong impact on the opinion we create of ourselves. Our self-talk builds and modifies our self-image, which in turn governs our performance.

Two points to remember about self-talk:

1. Self-talk is a form of an affirmation.

2. Self-talk is continuously positive or negative.

Because of those characteristics of self-talk and by virtue of its sheer volume, it can either enhance or undermine our written goals and affirmations.

⇨Self-talk helps us change our beliefs.

⇨Self-talk accumulates to build our habits, attitudes, beliefs, and expectations.

⇨We must control our self-talk or it will control us.

⇨When we affirm what we "don't want," we will get what we don't want instead of what we "do want."

The way we view ourselves determines how we act and perform. Since self-talk is either positive or negative, we can either talk ourselves into failure or into success.

> ***Whether you think you can or think you can't —***
> ***you are right.***

— **HENRY FORD**

It is estimated that each person has between 30,000 and 60,000 individual thoughts per day. Several studies on self-talk tell us that among the general population, more than 80 percent of our thoughts are negative. This means that as many as 48,000 negative thoughts per day are overwhelming our conscious thinking.

That's why it's so important to pay constant and vigilant attention to our self-talk, and ensure that it positively supports our goals and self-image.

Our words and thoughts must be handled carefully, with wisdom and understanding. Most of us keep ourselves so busy that we do not take the time to listen to the self-sabotaging language we regularly use with ourselves. And then we wonder why our lives are full of problems and do not bring us the fulfillment we desire.

R$_x$ercise

Set a timer for five minutes. During that time, write down every thought that comes into your mind. Don't censor your writing — simply write down whatever comes to mind. When the timer goes off, put your pen down and stop writing. You might be astonished to read what you have written.

_____

_____

_____

_____

_____

_____

_____

_____

_____

_____

---

5. Our Self-Talk Builds Our Self-Image

Self-image could be considered a mental picture we hold of ourselves. It is the way we see ourselves, internally and externally, as well as the way we view our interactions with people and the world around us. Self-image is heavily influenced by the images we hold of our bodies as we visualize them — face, weight, skin color, hair, feet, etc. It is also based upon our past conditioning and past experiences. Everyone has many self-images, that range from high in one area to low in another.

Our mind chatter, or inner self-talk, reflects our beliefs about our competency, skills, ability, knowledge, intelligence, creativity, and common sense. It also strongly influences our self-image. If others have repeatedly judged us in any of these areas, we eventually begin to agree with them and store those judgments in our subconscious. As we internalize these beliefs, they color our views of the world, the role we play in it, and the way we feel about and subsequently treat others and ourselves. We move toward and become like that which we think about.

**We move toward and become like
that which we think about.**

Self-image tends to stay fixed. When it is negative, it blocks us from seeing the truth about ourselves, and subsequently stifles our potential. Our self-image remains stagnant because our actions always mirror the way we picture ourselves. As a result, our mind chatter reflects these views and reinforces the existing self-image. This succession of events continues to repeat itself throughout our lives until we become self-aware enough to change it. The diagram below demonstrates this cycle.

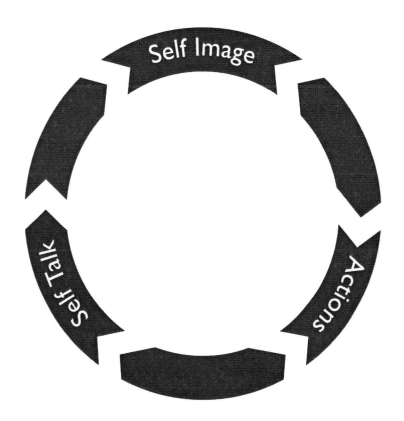

We can see a vivid example of the cycle described above in Mary, a student who thinks poorly of herself. Mary has always considered herself "dumb and stupid," yet somehow she gets an "A" on a test. However, even though she is encouraged by the "A," the next time she takes a test, regardless of how hard she studies beforehand, she is likely to find a way to sabotage herself and receive a "D" or an "F," thereby reinforcing the notion that her newfound self-image was simply a fluke. Mary is simply unable to sustain a new mental picture of herself as an excellent student. Her actions and self-talk continue to reinforce her long-held negative view of herself.

Think about the obesity syndrome in America. For many of us who are overweight, our unhappy image of ourselves causes us to quickly sabotage any diet or exercise strategies we undertake. The result is that our image of ourselves as "fat" remains dominant. The inevitable mind chatter after we "cheat" only reinforces how badly we feel about our weight and ourselves, and it starts the cycle all over again.

These examples illustrate how easy it is to talk oneself into or out of feelings of worthiness, and continuously perpetuate our weak self-images. Unfortunately, the formation of our self-image generally does not take into account the possibilities of what we might yet become, and therefore has the ability to block the use of our full potential.

Our self-image is our opinion of ourselves. Because we created it, only we can change it. Even though our self-image is our personal opinion, this opinion is based upon the opinions of other people — our parents, teachers, ministers, friends, and peers. Unfortunately, most of us make the mistake of believing these people.

The quickest way to be more effective is to raise our self-image and change our opinions about ourselves.

Self-image derives from one of two thought systems:

An ego thought system, which is an attack system based on fear.

A Higher Power thought system, which is based on love.

Love	Fear
Wisdom	Ego
Truth	False Truth
Sanity	Insanity
Peace of Mind	Attack
Unconditional Forgiveness	Conditional Forgiveness
Harmony	Critical
Abundance	Scarcity
Community	Separation

We can change our self-image by changing our reality. There are three parts to our process of thought: **Conscious**, **Subconscious, and Creative Subconscious**.

Conscious

⇨Our perception of our reality.

⇨How we personally understand and respond to what happens in our lives.

Subconscious

⇨Storehouse for the interpretation of what happens in our lives.

⇨Handles our automatic functions, like breathing and heartbeat.

Creative Subconscious

⇨Maintains our reality — it pushes us to act automatically.

⇨Based on our past experiences, we ask ourselves two questions:

Is this going to be good or bad for me?
When have I ever seen anything like this before?

Chapter Two
Fear: An Extension of the Ego Thought System

1. Fear Forms in the Subconscious

Our negative programming forms in the sub-conscious portion of our brain. Like a computer, the subconscious remembers everything that has ever happened to us during our lives, including the feelings and emotions attached to particular experiences. It stores our interpretation of our reality, and has complete and total recall. This storehouse of information determines our current thinking, attitudes, and actions in every situation in which we find ourselves. Our subconscious silently asks, "Where have I seen this situation before?" Then its retrieves the respective mental file and guides us to act based on the actions we have stored in that creaky, cerebral filing cabinet.

The types of relationships we create in our lives are perfect examples of how this process works. In my teenage years, I had several friendships that went sour and left me feeling unfulfilled and alone. These incidents, on top of my difficult family relationships, were quite uncomfortable and painful. Although I am a warm person and love to be with people, as time went on, I had difficulty letting myself develop and create trusting friendships, as I was fearful that the same experiences would repeat themselves. The memories and feelings about my previous encounters bubbled up from my subconscious and literally prevented me from taking new risks. My fearful mind had me believing that it was easier to be alone than open, or reveal myself in any way. Fortunately, I was able to override this frightful thinking with affirmations, and have learned how to be discerning in my relationships, which have created a whole new set of pictures and feelings in my subconscious.

If the majority of our experiences have been overwhelmingly negative, our self-talk becomes a constant barrage of demeaning, counterproductive, sabotaging things we repeat to ourselves on a daily basis. These are thoughts we reinforce, often without even realizing it. Most of us are totally unaware of the cycle we continue to perpetuate as we pepper our everyday conversation with negative statements about ourselves, our families, our friends, and our beliefs regarding world events.

R$_x$ercise

What are some of your biggest fears? Describe how you are frightened. Where did these fears originate? Are they rational? Are they self-imposed? What negative beliefs in your childhood led to their formation?

_____

_____

_____

_____

_____

_____

_____

_____

_____

_____

_____

_____

_____

2. Understanding the Effects of Fear

Before we can become self-affirming, we must understand the effects of negative thinking on our lives. It is essential to recognize that a good deal of our negativity stems from fear. Human beings are born with two fears for their protection: the fear of falling and the fear of loud noises. All other fear, such as the following, is learned conditioning.

1. Being alone; not having people around us, with us, near us.

2. A perceived inability to create the success and the "things" we want in our lives.

3. Losing what we already have accumulated and accomplished.

When we live in fear, we falsely believe that we are being deprived of the things that are necessary for our happiness; we may lose the things we already possess; and/or we are not deserving to have our needs met. These false thoughts keep us paralyzed and have a rebound effect on our lives. They prevent us from having, or cause us to lose all that we desire.

FEAR: False Evidence Appearing Real

3. The Myth of Security

A perfect example of fear-based thinking can be seen in our attitudes around saving or spending money. How many times have you thought you would feel more secure if you had enough money, clients/customers, or knowledge? Most of us honestly believe we would be secure if we had these things. Yet experience tells us that whenever we reach that goal we set of "enough money," we don't really feel secure and still feel we need to accumulate more. The same is true of other things we desire, such as a great job, perfect life partner, or renown in the community. None of these ever feel like enough, because deep down inside we do not feel like we are enough. When we live in fear, many of us deprive ourselves of the things we want or need because we feel guilty about having things.

One of my clients, Arden, hired me because she felt she was unable to earn enough money through her consulting business. Between sessions, she offered to pay me to review her resume and biography. Two days before our next scheduled session, Arden phoned to tell me she could not make it to our meeting. She felt she had gone beyond her financial limit for the month and had to deprive herself of a badly needed session.

As Arden and I discussed her cancellation, she could not understand how this behavior was an outgrowth of her fear around scarcity, and how such a fear was fueling her lack and limitation issues. It took several sessions before she comprehended that had she decided to attend that critical session rather than deprive herself, she would have demonstrated faith and a strong conviction that she would be able to attract more than enough money to pay for the extra session. When she finally did grasp this concept and spent the time and money on an extra session, three new opportunities presented themselves to her almost immediately.

4. Fear Is Learned in Childhood

Where did these fearful, untrusting, negative thoughts come from? Essentially, most of our fears and negative thoughts developed in childhood, through the conditioning we received from our teachers, parents, religions, and culture. Without consciously realizing it, these people and institutions taught us to think about life in terms of guilt and scarcity by promoting — even encouraging — unhealthy competition, resentment, selfishness, jealousy, and dishonesty. From the competition for grades and demands to prove ourselves on the athletic field, to sibling rivalry and the depiction of a punishing God who wants us to suffer, we were slowly indoctrinated into a culture of fear. It is not surprising then, that our habits, attitudes, and beliefs formed within this negative conditioning became our barriers to success. As adults, we continue to be bombarded with this negativity by the media, advertisements, spouses, bosses, relatives, and even some people we consider friends.

We are what we believe. Anyone who is exposed to negative thoughts, ideas, or concepts long enough will begin to believe them and incorporate them into their way of being. Our subjective negative environmental feedback becomes our truth. When a teacher continuously praises the same few children in his class while ridiculing the rest of the students for not doing "better," the ridiculed children begin to view themselves as unsuccessful, even failures.

Chapter Three
Negative Thinking
Is Unconsciously Passed
from Generation to Generation

In order to move past the fear-based programming ingrained in childhood and achieve our true potential, it is crucial to understand that as children, our parents and teachers were exposed to the same fears and negative thinking they unconsciously passed on to us. Most of the people in our lives were never allowed to think in terms of being true to themselves. In her book *What You Think of Me Is None of My Business*, Terry Cole-Whittaker tells us that the need of previous generations to please others created a boomerang effect which reverberates between our parents and ourselves, and is then passed on to our children as we become parents.

We can never truly have a positive self-image until we become honest with ourselves and understand that our own Higher Self is our best guide, rather than the gods we have made of our parents, teachers, bosses, and mentors.

R$_x$ercise

Make a list of those fears which hold you back the most from
succeeding in relationships, work, and with family. Who were they
learned from? What made you buy into this false thinking?

_____

_____

_____

_____

_____

_____

_____

_____

_____

_____

_____

_____

Reconsider your list of fears. If you were to make the decision to
ACCEPT your life as it is, and believe the Universe will support
you in having everything you need to be happy, which of these
fears can you begin to release at this moment? What specific
actions are you willing to take to conquer the other fears (i.e.,
affirmations, listen to and/or read spiritual tapes and books, work
with a coach)?

_____

_____

_____

_____

_____

_____

_____

_____

_____

_____

_____

_____

_____

_____

1. Criticism of Others Is an Extension of Our Self-Loathing

It is important to recognize that when we criticize others, we really are disparaging ourselves. Criticism of others is an outgrowth of our own unhappiness and negative thoughts. Our inability to experience ourselves in a positive light causes us to project our negative feelings onto others. By criticizing and blaming others, we can delay or avoid feeling the discomfort of our dissatisfaction with ourselves.

Whittaker explains, "As criticizers, we suppress people mentally, spiritually, and physically, resulting in their inability to believe in themselves. They literally believe they have done something wrong. When we are able to stop using others to carry our own dissatisfaction with ourselves, which came from our suppressors, and are willing to own our unhappiness and do something about it, then we will stop the cycle of passing guilt from one to another."

As with everything, the Law of Attraction causes this form of negative energy to bounce back to us, continually reinforcing our negative feelings, attitudes, and beliefs. We will never be able to rid ourselves of these conditioned feelings of self-hate and self-denial as long as we continue to allow ourselves to be motivated from a place of criticism and blame. A vicious cycle of unhappiness forms which cannot and will not stop until we are able to look deep inside ourselves and be completely honest with ourselves and own our truth.

Go back to the radio example. Remember, you can only be in sync with one frequency at a time. As long as you are unable to line up your day-to-day thoughts with your desires, it will be impossible to synchronize these energies and manifest what you want. Negative thinking prevents us from being on the same vibration or wavelength as our wishes. The Law of Attraction will not let you think one way and attract in a different way. The laws of the Universe are immutable — they are constant and never change. If you are out of vibrational alignment with your desires, you will never achieve them, no matter how hard you try. If they do come to you, in spite of the vibrational misalignment, they will remain with you only fleetingly.

R$_x$ercise

1.) For the next week, listen to yourself as you speak to others. Observe how many times you make self-deprecating remarks, criticize, or play the blame game. Write down what you notice each day, as it occurs. Try to determine what feelings caused you to make these remarks. Allow yourself to dig deep.

2.) Once you are able to uncover the feelings that caused you to blame, criticize and ridicule others, refer back to the scenarios you wrote about and rewrite them with behavior that reflects support, honesty, and respect for the individuals and situations you described.

_____

_____

_____

_____

_____

_____

_____

_____

_____

_____

_____

_____

_____

_____

2. Letting Go of the Need to be Perfect

Perfection is a true killer of ideas and creativity. It not only prevents us from living in possibility and spontaneity, it depletes our ability to learn new skills and be innovative at the same time. Our fear of failing and not being good enough becomes a self-fulfilling prophecy because it ties up and blocks our energy. This causes us to "go in circles," getting nowhere fast, and accomplishing far less than we had hoped we would.

We all know life is not perfect. A mistake is either a wrong action or an error due to ignorance. Healing the negative behavior of perfection comes from recognizing our mistakes, learning from them, and making corrections or deciding how we can do it differently if confronted with the same type of situation. The natural learning condition of all human beings is trial and error, and mistakes are the most natural part of growth. Our errors are useful, as they allow us to correct our actions.

We can use self-talk such as, "Next time, I intend to . . ." or "Isn't that interesting!" to change our responses to mistakes. When we understand that the next time, or the time after, we will still not do it perfectly, we will make greater and quicker improvements to whatever circumstances might confront us. The beauty of this process is that we begin to see ourselves as people who are constantly growing while gaining new skills and knowledge to help us live more productively and harmoniously.

While working with a client recently, I had a great "aha" moment. Jeff and one other partner had just bought out the senior monetary partner, Ryan, from a floundering mid-size manufacturing firm. Jeff had spent the last six months getting up to speed, going through a major learning curve in the areas that Ryan was overseeing. In order to make the transition easier, he hired a consultant with excellent skills to add to his knowledge of the systems in those departments and provide insight for their improvement.

Jeff was continually feeling frustrated over the decisions he was making in this part of the business, especially when the consultant showed him they would be detrimental to operations and profit. By the time we spoke about this, he was very upset with himself and his "mind-chatter" was out of control. Upon further investigation, Jeff revealed to me that this happened to him quite frequently. After some discussion, I gleaned this was all about perfection and I shared this with him. It took more explanation, but he finally understood that he was comparing himself to the consultant and not allowing himself the time needed to learn the systems in these departments. It was no accident that Jeff was behaving in this manner. Even though he understood perfection and had been reading about it, something deeper came to light.

For years he had what I call, "early morning fear." Jeff found himself scared to start the day, and full of major butterflies in the pit of his stomach. Now that he was changing so much of his thinking, he really wanted to stop being frightened. We analyzed it to death, and although there was some improvement, the fear did not disappear. I finally made the decision to tell Jeff that he needed to accept this fear and pray that it would leave him.

It worked! Within a few weeks, Jeff had an epiphany. He saw the reasons for his morning fear clearly. He had been waking up each day worried about being perfect. He finally recognized that he was petrified of not being perfect with everyone he encountered, but especially himself, before he had even slipped out of bed. Because of his upbringing, this made sense to him. His parents and private school teachers were expecting constant perfection, and if he didn't achieve it, he paid a heavy price of being severely criticized and shamed.

No one had ever taught him that when we are learning, it is a process. Everything he did had to be perfect — from the minute he was asked to do something — and many times very little direction was given on how to best accomplish the task. Jeff shared that his parents rarely took the time to explain things. In fact, they would judge and criticize his actions almost constantly.

Jeff related that in school, his teachers made As and 100s the only scores acceptable. If he received a low grade on a test or quiz, the teacher might go over the right answers, but no one took the time to truly teach him or the other students the benefit of making mistakes and learning from them. I believe this way of thinking is foreign to most people. Our society and approach to education does not promote risk taking and making mistakes as a way to succeed and move forward. Can you imagine how different our education system would be if this method of thinking was adopted?

When you have been brought up to believe that all you do must be perfect, it becomes a terrible trap. As soon as you make a mistake, your "mind-chatter" becomes berating and demeaning. It is a reflection of those voices you heard, and still hear today from people screaming the need for you to be perfect. The truth is that no one can do anything perfectly. There will always be room for improvement, no matter how well we can do something. We can only accept what we have accomplished in the moment, and know that we have the ability to do it differently and better if it doesn't work for us. It takes courage, persistence, and hours of practice to do anything well. Ask successful athletes how they have achieved success and you will hear about the years of hard work they put in to learn their sport.

Has anyone ever told you it was okay to make a mistake? The answer is probably no. It is okay to make mistakes. That is how we learn and improve. There is no other way. It is not shameful to ask for help, whether to learn how to do something or improve on it. In Think and Grow Rich, Napoleon Hill tells us about the mastermind: "No two minds ever come together without, thereby, creating a third, invisible, intangible force which may be likened to a third mind." We know the mind is energy and has great power. Therefore when two or more minds come together, the power multiplies.

Successful people have courage and are willing to take risks because they do not fear making mistakes. They know that their mistakes will teach them how to move forward and make something work. The old story about Thomas Alva Edison could not provide a better example. This is a man who did not give up, but accepted his mistakes and kept his passion strong. He saw his mistakes as steps toward taking improved action. And of course, that is how he developed the light bulb.

If your visions or affirmations are not working, go back to the drawing board and determine what is holding you back. We don't give up because they don't work the first, second, or tenth time. When we accept that our happiness comes from our own growth, at our own pace, making as many mistakes as we need, then we have given up perfection for a life of success.

Follow this four-step process when you make a mistake:

1. Pinpoint what did not work. Write down, if possible, your part in making the error, especially if it involves other people.

2. Think about what you would do differently now that you know the results of your actions. If appropriate, share this with the others involved. Do not ignore it or be untruthful; own up to it immediately.

3. Forgive yourself for making the mistake and affirm that the next time you will do it differently…

4. Hand it over to your Higher Power and visualize yourself doing it differently.

R$_x$ercise

1.) Describe how you handle making mistakes. What is your "mind-chatter" like after you've made an error?

_____

_____

_____

_____

_____

_____

_____

_____

_____

_____

_____

_____

_____

_____

_____

_____

_____

2.) In your journal, use the four steps above to work through a major mistake you made recently.

3.) Read as many books as you can about famous people who have persevered and become successful.

3. Procrastination is Just Another Form of Fear

Procrastination is very similar to perfection. It is a time waster and keeps us from reaching our goals. It is a clear statement of "I am not worthy." And it is a fear of performance. Louise Hay tells us in You Can Heal Your Life that, "most people who procrastinate will spend a lot of time and energy berating themselves for procrastinating. They will call themselves lazy and generally will make themselves out to feel they are bad persons."

We delay our actions by doing something other than what we plan to do and waste time. Most people spend a great deal of time keeping far too busy. Our society is into multi-tasking to get it all done. People brag that they work 24/7. This is the most interesting form of procrastination, as it's all about fear — fear of failure, rejection, what others think, not being ready to change, letting our "secrets" out, not being enough, and intimacy. If you look closely, most of these people are not succeeding. In fact, they are doing very little well because they are spread so thin and constantly in a state of exhaustion. The bottom line is that they are miserable and refuse to spend the time figuring out how to change it.

R$_x$ercise

1.) Make a list of all the ways you procrastinate. Be honest with yourself.

2.) Write about your feelings of unworthiness and how they relate to your list.

3.) Create an affirmation that helps you support your worthiness. One I use with clients all the time is, "I am enough, I do enough, I have enough." Later on, you will learn how to effectively use affirmations.

_____

_____

_____

_____

_____

_____

_____

_____

_____

_____

_____

_____

_____

_____

4. Creating Self-Esteem — Learning How to Set Boundaries for Yourself and Others

Fear is the culprit behind people being dishonest. If you dig deep enough, you will find that people are untruthful because they are afraid of the consequences — real or imagined — that will occur if they are honest. In addition, most people do not realize that purposefully omitting important information is a form of dishonesty. Dishonesty by omission is not being truthful with someone about our real feelings over an issue or interaction. This not only prevents the receiver from having the necessary information that may help to change the situation, but it disempowers the person who is not being entirely truthful. Furthermore, if an individual does not know or understand what "you need" to make a situation better, the problem goes unresolved and weakens the situation or relationship.

Telling others "the whole truth" is an empowering action because we free ourselves of negative energy and clear the path for positive and good things to happen. Use the method described below to express your true thoughts, feelings, and needs. I know you will see a difference in how others respond to you and how you feel about yourself.

1. Tell the other person your truth by describing the feelings or attitudes you are experiencing, seeing, or hearing that are making you feel uncomfortable. Always use the words "I feel, I hear, I see" and keep it in the first person.

2. Never use the words "you did this" or "you made me feel" as they come across as an attack and typically provoke a defensive response. It is best to say, "When I heard you say" or "when I saw you do," "I experienced..." (then describe the feelings, such as anger, disappointment, etc.).

3. Finish the interaction by describing "what you need" to improve the situation. This step is most important. By letting someone know what is bothering you without telling him or her what you need, you leave out the most important step in the process, you literally short circuit the possibility of resolving the situation.

4. Recognize that while you may not get everything you need, you will have opened up the conversation for new solutions and compromises that can create a win-win for all involved.

I cannot think of a client that I have worked with who has not needed to work on setting boundaries with their spouse, friends, children, parents and/or employers. Our society has not taught us how to properly empower each other and ourselves. Once we learn how to honestly let others know our "truth" and "needs," we open ourselves up to incredible personal power, respect, and intimacy with others — intimacy and understanding that can only be created through honesty.

Chapter Four
Symptoms and Outcomes
of Negative Thinking

1. The Symptoms

Some ways in which we punish ourselves for not allowing ourselves to live freely are:

- Overworking and not taking time to enjoy the fruits of our labor.
- Living in self-denial and unnecessary austerity.
- Being constantly afraid to let our guard down and relax, lest someone else beat us to that elusive happiness or success.

Let's look at other symptoms that are the result of internalizing all this negative self-talk. A few of the main ones include:

Scarcity

Lack and limitation are our everyday guidelines for living. We are unable to see the richness of the Universe and never feel we are enough, do enough, or have enough. It always feels as if everyone else has more, in terms of success, money, and love.

Pessimism

Our self-defeating view of ourselves leads us to see the whole world in a negative light. We see nothing through a positive lens and can't be convinced that life holds many wonderful opportunities for us. We no longer believe success is an option for us and are no longer willing to take an optimistic position as we look toward the future. We see only failure, gloom, and heartbreak on the horizon.

Anger

We are unable to stay calm in most situations, and even the smallest things irritate us. More often than not, we are full of rage and fury. We are inappropriately antagonistic towards others. We are resentful and find forgiveness difficult, if not impossible.

Self-Pity

We have come to feel so sorry for ourselves and how life has treated us that we become the hosts of our own "pity parties." We get so lost in self-sorrow, regrets, remorse, and pity that we refuse to be shaken or changed. We actually begin to believe that no one will notice us unless they can feel sorry for us.

Immobilization

Our rigid negative belief systems hold us back from taking risks in life —preventing us from wanting to make changes, freezing our feelings into negative patterns, and convincing us

that our only role in life is to be victimized by those who intend
to hurt us.

The Impenetrable Shield

We create invisible shields, impossible for others to either see
or penetrate. When people approach us to try and involve us, we
zap them with our shields and they back off or flee altogether.
Our shields work so subtly that at times we don't even know they
exist, and we get confused when people we really care about pull
away from us. Our shields can take the form of coldness, sarcasm,
addiction, aloofness, unwillingness to change or take a risk,
attacking out of fear of being taken advantage of, resistance to
intimacy, arrogance, timidity, or any other feeling that keeps us
from connecting emotionally with another person.

Cynicism

We take the cynical "yes, but . . ." approach toward every
suggestion for change in our lives. We doubt the sincerity,
kindness, and love of others who still care enough to try to help
us. We create a barrier of cynicism to block them out, thus
convincing ourselves when they ultimately leave us that they
never really cared in the first place.

Fulfillment of the Prophecy

We've become so accustomed to predicting the worst, that at
some subconscious level we begin working to achieve the worst.
We succeed in fulfilling our negative prophecies of failure,
rejection, loss, disapproval, and other tragic outcomes.

Fault Finding

We are critical and perfectionistic with ourselves and others.
It is difficult for us to see the good in people and the world

around us. We are afraid to make mistakes, feeling we will be viewed as weak if we do.

Conditional Forgiveness

Anything we do for another has a qualification attached to it. We are unable to give freely of our time, love, or money to our friends, family, or the world at large.

Depression

Because of the anger, resentment, rage, hurt, disappointment, disillusionment, and suffering we experience as a result of our negative self-talk, we become good candidates for firm and long-lasting depression. Our emotions can become so rigid and constricted that we can become programmed with a deep sense of melancholy and a loss of hope. At this stage, we become candidates for mental health intervention, before the depression reaches the despair level and we become more self-destructive, possibly physically ill, or even suicidal.

R$_x$ercise

Review each of the above-mentioned character traits and examples of behaviors that keep us blocked and prevent us from being completely truthful with ourselves. How do these self-defeating behaviors show up in your life?

_____

_____

_____

_____

_____

_____

_____

_____

_____

_____

_____

_____

_____

_____

_____

_____

R$_x$ercise

In which areas of your life do you tend to create self-sabotage? How can you begin to revise your thinking to allow for the possibility that you might be able to achieve immense success?

_____

_____

_____

_____

_____

_____

_____

_____

_____

The only way we can alter how we feel about ourselves is by first observing our actions, words, and thoughts while noticing the circumstances in which they are occurring. If we do this consistently, a new habit of self-observation will develop. As time goes on, we become more conscious of what we are doing and we begin to break down the denial we have allowed ourselves to live in. At first we may only become aware of our personal feelings and the appropriateness of how we have dealt with a certain situation or interaction with others after the fact. Eventually we begin to catch ourselves as these situations are happening, and then magically stop ourselves before we act out the misguided behavior or say something inappropriate. Simultaneously, we begin to gain insight into the reasons we are thinking or behaving in a manner which is hurting us. When this happens, we start to see ourselves differently, we feel more self-confident, and we build our self-esteem.

Before any effective change will stick, we must be able to be totally honest with ourselves. This is where mentors and support systems can be very helpful. Many times they can see what we have trouble seeing about ourselves and can provide us with their perceptions and suggestions for change. As we go through this process, we can rid ourselves of false beliefs that have followed us since our childhood. Once we are able to think differently about ourselves and our world, we can begin to love and respect ourselves in new, enriching ways.

As we become more conscious of our negative self-talk and subsequent behaviors, we must remain alert to the many ways we block ourselves from being self-aware, thereby perpetuating the cycle that strengthens a damaged self-image. We must remember that any feelings of anger, resentment, or hostility arising after we see the cost of our actions are by-products and reinforcements of this negative self-image cycle. Let's take a closer look at some of the ways we keep ourselves unconscious.

2. Victim Thinking Stunts Our Personal Development

When we view ourselves as victims of others' behaviors, we become immobilized and emotionally stunted. The fastest way to shift out of this thought process is to remember that we have actually made a choice to give away our power or allow ourselves to be suppressed.

Douglas, a senior level technical specialist, contacted me because he had just been passed over for a promotion to senior vice-president in his organization. His managers, peers, and subordinates had just completed a thorough "360" company review, during which Douglas learned that although he was seen as quite bright and knowledgeable, everyone felt that he was very defensive and not open to suggestions.

Following the review, I had the opportunity to shadow Douglas on his job and see him in action. I saw firsthand that Douglas did have a very difficult time listening to others state their opinions. Fortunately, once he was able to take ownership of this behavior, he was willing to step back, observe himself, and accept my suggestions to help him change his behavior.

He began by exploring why he was so defensive, and discovered that although his father loved him, he constantly expected perfection from Douglas. No matter how hard Douglas tried to please his dad, it never was quite right or enough. In response, Douglas had become an overachiever, and very sensitive to the comments of others because he was so incredibly hard on himself.

Douglas worked on releasing his need to see himself as a victim or a failure when he made the same human mistakes we all make, and slowly opened to letting others assist and support him. Gradually, he began to understand that the energy of two minds is greater than one, and he began to realistically see other people as collaborators rather than controllers. Today he is a thriving senior vice-president of development.

R$_x$ercise

Do you have a difficult time accepting feedback or suggestions? Do you constantly find fault with others, but have a difficult time celebrating their successes? What can you do to begin to allow for the possibility that others (coworkers, bosses, spouse, friends, family, business partners) might actually be collaborators rather than controllers?

_____

_____

_____

_____

_____

_____

_____

_____

_____

_____

_____

_____

3. "To Compare Is to Despair"

A close cousin to victimhood is that old, ugly, green monster — jealousy, another symptom of poor self-image. When we allow ourselves to wallow in jealousy toward others we perceive to be luckier, wealthier, better looking, more popular, smarter, more talented, more creative, and generally happier and more successful than ourselves, feelings of inferiority can begin to consume us. As a result, we embody the belief that no matter what we do in life, it will never be good enough to get us where others are.

Once we understand the origins of our negative self-talk and self-image, we can change them by using affirmations to create positive, new self-talk. A wonderful affirmation for jealousy is: "To compare is to despair." Some of my clients have shared that these five little words have helped them on numerous occasions to climb out of the "pity pot" during important moments when standing up for their beliefs and exhibiting self-confidence was paramount to their success. Comparing ourselves in any way to another person or situation is a death knell for our individuality, self-esteem, and personal belief systems.

R$_x$ercise

What are the circumstances or occasions that often serve to awaken your green-eyed monster? How can you reevaluate your perspective about the situations, people, or material objects that seem to trigger your feelings of jealousy? What personal affirmation(s) can you create to offset those envious feelings when they arise?

_____

_____

---

4. Hypersensitivity to Mistakes

Much like our response to perceived infractions committed against us by others, we can become overwhelmed by feelings of guilt over real or imagined wrongs we have committed against others. We can get caught up in worrying about what others think of us, the first impressions we create, and pleasing people.

The fact is that because we're human, we're going to screw up — it's practically encoded into our DNA. However, we can use our mistakes as learning opportunities, or we can anguish over them and allow them to destroy our self-image. We need to remind ourselves that many times mistakes are good, not bad. By making mistakes we grow and get useful insights into the reasons behind our actions.

As people analyze their responses to mistakes, they often find their answers linked to childhood experiences of being pressed to live according to their parents' wishes. Because their own free will was not supported, they never learned it was okay to make a mistake. In an echo of their childhood behavior, they have a difficult time making decisions and owning them, particularly if those decisions are incorrect. Yet, they continue to give away their power to others, not realizing that most of the time we are our own worst critics. The good news is that every one of us can learn to be honest with ourselves and face our demons. Once we do this, we become free, and can then in turn, help others become free too.

R$_x$ercise

Have there been times in your life when you have blown your part in a mistake out of proportion? Did you feel ashamed and make excuses, or cover up the mistake? Did that correct the error and make you feel better, or exacerbate the situation? What new thought or belief can you entertain to help you own your next mistake, learn from it, and move on?

_____

_____

_____

_____

_____

_____

_____

_____

_____

_____

_____

_____

_____

5. Always Seeking Validation

On the opposite side of the coin from always feeling responsible for mistakes, missteps, and miscues is the continual need to be validated by others. Sometimes we become dependent on constant recognition and validation from someone else, whether that someone is a spouse, parent, family member, colleague, boss, friend, minister, community organization, or professional affiliation.

Validation and approval are human needs — each one of us requires some form of positive feedback at times. However, seeking external validation becomes dangerous when we are so obsessed with the need for recognition of our worth, competency, beauty, and overall goodness that if others do not meet that need for us — because they are unwilling, unable, or uninformed — we spiral into a depressive vortex of unworthiness and destructive self-talk. Once we can accept that no one except our own higher self will ever fill our needs, we reach a milestone in learning and embodying self-reliance. Behind the manifestation of everything we need and desire is our Higher Power — our one true source.

Sharon grew up in an alcoholic home. Although her father was a functioning alcoholic and quite successful, this was a man who always found ways to sabotage the family so they would remain dependent on him. He constantly needed to be the center of attention. As a result, Sharon grew up never feeling safe and trusting of herself, especially around her father. As she grew older, she turned to men who were controlling and wanted them to "take care of her." She became a victim in these relationships and was continuously disappointed at the results. Once Sharon recognized and understood her fear of being self-reliant, she slowly began to recognize that she always had a choice to take actions that would empower her and no longer keep her trapped in her old habits. Her crowning moment came when she was able to tell her father to stop minimizing her capabilities and to not say anything to her that wasn't positive. The results were astonishing! He began to show total respect for Sharon, and she began to take ownership for all aspects of her life, including advancing her career.

R$_x$ercise

How often do you find yourself in the position of seeking external validation? What does this praise, recognition, or a pat on the back from others do for you? What steps can you take to begin to feel good enough, special enough, and worthy enough just because you're you — without needing an outside source as your constant champion or cheering squad?

_____

_____

_____

_____

_____

_____

_____

_____

_____

_____

_____

_____

_____

6. The Value of Finding a Mentor or Coach

There is a difference between validation and support. Most people need a minimum of five to six people they can rely on for assistance and support in the different areas of their lives. In fact, virtually every person who has achieved a significant level of success has had different mentors and coaches along their journey. There's no reason why each one of us cannot find mentors in our own lives . . . people who have done the things we aspire to do, or, better yet, people who are actually doing the things we aspire to do. The greatest gift we can give ourselves — beyond total honesty — is to find another person who has walked this journey and allow them to mentor us during the difficult times.

We must remember, however, that while these mentors are guides to help us fulfill our needs, they are not the sources. If we are still in a serious state of depression, even after finding and working with a mentor, we must critically examine our profound level of self-hate and get the necessary professional help to develop the self-love we so richly deserve.

Regardless of whether or not we decide to work with a mentor, we still must consistently use affirmations to help us reprogram our thinking and learn how to positively acknowledge ourselves. The use of affirmations and a full understanding of the Law of Attraction will enable us to create more love for ourselves and a new relationship with our Higher Power. Over time, following this prescription will help us recognize our self-worth and increase our self-esteem, and we will learn that we can attract everything we desire to us.

R$_x$ercise

Make a list of the people in your life who support you unconditionally. They can be friends, family members, your minister, your letter carrier, your hair dresser . . . anyone who helps you stay focused and positive, who supports your goals and dreams, or who has been where you aspire to go. This may be a challenge for you, particularly if you've spent the most recent part of your life attracting people who continue to validate your feelings of low self-worth. If you're reading this book though, you are clearly ready to make a change. Somewhere, someone in your life is offering you a positive ray of hope. If you want one specific mentor, do some journaling around who you might like that person to be. What do they do for a living? Where do they live? Are they similar to or different from you? How could you set out to find such a mentor?

_____

_____

_____

_____

_____

_____

_____

_____

_____

_____

_____

_____

7. The "What If?" Trap

Sometimes our fear and resulting mind chatter takes the form of "what if?" We can allow ourselves to become haunted by worry and negative prophecies about our future, our successes, our failures, our relationships, our families, our health, or ourselves. Such doom and gloom can become a huge obstacle, creating an unnecessary struggle in our search for happiness and success. Next time, instead of making the "what if" a negative, how about making it a positive? Instead of saying, "What if my boss hates my presentation?" ask, "What if my boss loves my presentation?" And then visualize the positive outcome that results.

R$_x$ercise

Pay attention to how often you catch yourself in "what if?" thinking or surround yourself with "buts." Are these real worries, or merely excuses to continue living in your safe but miserable comfort zone? What affirmation or positive thought can you use to replace the "what ifs" and "buts" so they don't destroy your mental stability? How can you rephrase your "what ifs" and "buts" in positive, supportive language?

_____

_____

_____

_____

_____

_____

_____

_____

_____

_____

_____

_____

8. The Burden of Overresponsibility

We sometimes become overwhelmed by the overresponsibility with which we burden ourselves. This self-sabotaging behavior can develop from the perception that others in our lives will never be able to fully take care of themselves and that we are "responsible" for them, no matter what. This belief is, in fact, a lie and a form of manipulation by both the giver and the receiver. As each one performs their part in the dance of codependence, neither one really achieves self-reliance.

None of us were put on this earth to take care of the helpless. It is an impossible task and one at which we can never succeed. Look at any addict and you will see a person who cannot recover from their disease until they recognize that they alone are the only ones who can decide to stop their addictive behavior. No amount of cajoling and caretaking by their overburdened families and loved ones will ever make a difference until the user/taker/receiver decides to stop using/taking/receiving. We can only change our own behavior.

If givers continue to give in search of that ever-elusive validation, they eventually become emotionally empty, physically sick, or crazy. The tragedy is that all lose. Only when the caretaker gets strong enough to decide that perhaps giving is not in his or her own best interest, can the paradigm shift and a new perspective begin to take hold.

R~x~ercise

Are there areas in your life where you are overgenerous or you overcommit in order to feel worthy and important? What would happen if you slowly decided to start giving less but doing more to take care of your own self? How would your relationships change? How would those changes affect your life? Can you make a decision today to give a little less to everyone else and a little more to yourself?

_____

_____

_____

_____

_____

_____

_____

_____

_____

_____

_____

_____

_____

_____

_____

_____

_____

_____

9. Missing the Present to Live in the Past or the Future

Negative programming can relate to past failures or poor performances, the mental recordings of which we systematically replay again and again in our minds. Concentrating on past failures can produce negative attitudes about our potential future successes, thereby influencing our motivation, effort, and drive to attain our goals. By remaining focused on the past, we can create such dread and fear about the future that we falsely convince ourselves we do not have what it takes to move forward. We become so certain we will fail that we procrastinate in setting goals or attempting the actions that will bring new achievements.

On the other hand, we can become so entrenched in thoughts of the future that we are unable to take the steps today that will actually get us there. We sometimes live in a fantasy or dream world of "someday" and "if only" — completely failing to realize that if we would simply stay in the present and take small action steps, those dreams could and would become reality.

We can allow ourselves to become prisoners of our pasts or our futures, or we can make the conscious decision to live in the now. When you come to understand that at every moment you have the ability to start over and begin creating the life you want by reprogramming your thoughts and beliefs, you will have transcended your old belief system. It is at this point you accept that there is a loving, powerful energy force that conspires to support you every inch of the way.

R$_x$ercise

How often do you sabotage your present-moment happiness because you return to memories of failure or defeat? How often do you fantasize about a dream future that seems unattainable or too good to be true? What affirmation could you create to use when you find yourself drifting from the present into the past or the future? How could you stay present-focused and change your old belief systems?

_____

_____

_____

_____

_____

_____

_____

_____

_____

_____

_____

The only way out of our old, negative patterns of living in the past or the future, or our dependency on others is by doing the internal work of understanding how the negative beliefs were formed in the first place. Once we can accept the falseness of the beliefs that have decimated our self-worth, we become ready to take the actions necessary to create new habits, attitudes, and beliefs that will move us forward, push us to success, and enable us to reach our potential.

You have a choice to erase the old mental tapes and conditioning and record new ones. Are you willing to make this choice?

Chapter Five
Symptoms and Outcomes
of Living Freely

1. The Symptoms of Living Freely

Peace of Mind

We wake up each day with a sense of trust and calm, and feel confident that our higher self will supply everything we need. Our approach to life is tranquil and quiet. We see all of life as harmonious and full of serenity, and know that no matter how difficult things seem to be, there will be a good result.

Truth

We are always honest with ourselves and others. We never criticize, blame, or gossip because we recognize these behaviors will come back to us through the Law of Attraction. We understand that when things go wrong we must look at our part and make amends and corrections.

Unconditional Forgiveness

We give unqualified support to those who need it and expect nothing in return. We are supportive and understanding of each other's differences. We surrender the need to be right in all situations.

Love Seeking

We understand that love is God, and it is our true, eternal nature. We come from a place of humility, and recognize the internal goodness of humanity. We realize that if we fulfill our needs, we will be able to demonstrate love and compassion to everyone we meet.

Unity

We see that people are not separate from each other, but rather are eternally and spiritually united. We understand that we are all connected to something greater than ourselves. We know that we are all one and realize that what we think and do can and will affect everyone and the earth around us.

Abundance

We acknowledge that our Creator is the endless source for love and supply — that there is no such thing as scarcity in the Universe. We recognize that money and possessions do not make us happy, but that happiness and love will bring us everything we need, and more. We know that feeling unworthy and undeserving only makes us small — we deserve to prosper because we originated from the inexhaustible supply of our Higher Power.

Gratitude

We are grateful for everything we have — freedom, health, family, love, our bodies, our work, and more. We constantly thank our Higher Power for the large and small gifts that appear on a daily basis. We understand our authentic connection with our Higher Power and know that our purpose is one of service.

Humility

We comprehend that our ego is a very small part of our brain but has a very loud voice that is totally deceptive. We recognize that we can be very successful and prosperous without having to take advantage of others or be dishonest. Our modesty and unassuming nature make us attractive to others and prevents us from assuming arrogant behavior.

R$_x$ercise

Drawing from the list on pages 79-81, make a new list of the positive practices you can begin to implement that will keep you alert and aware of old, negative patterns and behaviors. Which of these self-affirming habits can you commit to trying out, starting today?

_____

_____

_____

_____

_____

_____

_____

_____

_____

2. Making Time for Journaling

Journaling is one of the best ways to discover your innermost feelings and desires and give yourself a new sense of freedom. I have been journaling for the past 15 years using a method that I call "Left Hand-Right Hand Journaling." It requires patience to learn, but once you practice it for several weeks, you'll be hooked on using it to get the answers you're searching for. Take the time to buy a notebook or diary that will be special for you. Then search out an area in your home where you will be undisturbed and make it your sacred space to be used just for meditating and journaling. By the way, journaling is a form of meditation and has always worked for me.

Left Hand-Right Hand Journaling

1. In your notebook, write the words "Dear Little _____" (put your name in the space) at the top of the page in your dominant hand. Since most people are right-handed, this will most likely be with your right hand.

2. Continuing with your dominant hand, write the question, "How are you feeling today?" on the next line.

3. Answer this question with your other hand, which for most people will be their left hand. At first your writing will be quite illegible. That is perfectly okay. Within a short period it will become clearer and clearer.

4. Write for as long as you need to, usually 10–15 minutes. There is no right or wrong here. If you feel resistance,

try to write about it. For most people it is natural not to initially want to go deep and experience their feelings. Be patient and let yourself build up to it.

5. After you have written for a while, write the words "Dear Little One," or something else endearing, in your dominant hand. Then summarize what you have written in your less dominant hand, praising yourself for being honest, or for any success you have accomplished, which includes attempting this type of journaling. Over time, you will get better at finding ways to write in more loving ways to yourself. Sign your writing with the word "Love," followed by your name.

Go ahead, give it a try.

Part II

Chapter One
Taking Command of Your Life

1. Actual Experience versus Imagined Experience

All of us have thoughts that limit us, even those who are successful. The key to releasing them is seeing that they are false beliefs which have been programmed into us by our environment. Only when we are willing to dare to think differently will we be able to reprogram our subconscious and create new visions and plans for our lives.

Study after study has shown that the subconscious mind cannot tell the difference between an actual experience and a vividly imagined experience. Let's look at the following examples.

There is a popular story about some scientists in California who conducted an experiment with the savage barracuda and its natural prey, the Spanish mackerel. They put both species of fish into a large tank on either side of a Plexiglas barrier. Initially the barracuda could see the mackerel in the tank, and naturally tried to attack it, but was stopped by the Plexiglas barrier. Continually trying to attack, it kept bumping into the divider. Eventually, the barracuda learned that the barrier was there and it stopped trying to get to the mackerel. After several weeks, the partition was removed. What do you think happened? Nothing. The barracuda had been programmed to not even try to reach the mackerel, so these two sworn enemies were able to live side by side.

This experiment demonstrates two important points. The first is that repeated reminders of how we cannot do something easily become beliefs that hold us back. The barracuda came to believe it could not reach the mackerel, so it no longer even tried. The second lesson from the experiment is that even the most intrinsic conditioning can be changed — it is possible to grow into a completely new way of thinking.

Here's another example:

A group of college athletes was divided into three smaller subgroups — group A, group B, and group C. Group A went to the gym every day and practiced shooting foul shots. The athletes in group B sat in a room every day, closed their eyes, and visualized themselves successfully making foul shots. Group C did nothing outside of their usual practice routine. After 30 days, each group was tested to see how much it had improved in making foul shots compared to its initial performance. The results were interesting. The group that did nothing beyond their normal routine did not significantly change, the group that went to gym every day improved by 24 percent, and the group that visualized improving their shooting increased their performance by 23 percent.

Imagine improving your performance by a significant margin simply by seeing mental pictures of yourself performing that behavior well! This doesn't just work for college athletes — it can work in your life too. These studies, and many others like them, prove that by vividly imagining an action, we can imprint it on our minds just the same as if we had undergone the genuine, authentic experience.

Every experience we have is our personal perception of that experience. Ask for details from three people who have witnessed a crime or accident and you will get three very different versions of the story because of their individual perceptions. The fact is, we create our reality from the feelings and thoughts we have about our life experiences.

2. Letting Go of the Old Precedes All Change

In order for any change or growth to occur, there must first be a letting go, a surrender. Most people think of surrender as a loss of freedom, a defeat, or a weakness. The primary definition of change, however, is to give something up in order to get something else. Only when you can accept that your old ways and patterns are no longer serving you will you be able to let go of your old behaviors and perceptions, and become open to embracing new ones.

All permanent and lasting change first begins inside you and works its way out. According to Wayne Dyer, "If you consider all the teachings of the spiritual masters, they all say the same thing: 'The kingdom of heaven is within.'" In order for effective change to occur, you must look within to get to the root of all your issues, discomforts, doubts, and old beliefs. And you must go inside of yourself to discover your dreams and get answers.

Unfortunately, most people do not draw into their lives what is rightfully theirs. They never quite attract what they desire because deep down they believe that if it were to happen, it would be "too good to be true." On the other hand, it never occurs to truly successful people that something cannot be done. These people always feel successful and live with the expectancy that something wonderful will happen — and it invariably does.

Ultimately, we are our own puppet masters, always pulling our own strings. It is so important to remain aware that our minds vibrate and constantly attract exactly what we are thinking about. When you feel successful, you attract success. Likewise, if you feel poor, you experience poverty.

Joan, a single mother, had been working for a year on commission as an investment counselor for a major bank. Due to issues that kept cropping up for her, Joan was having trouble staying motivated and doing the necessary cold calling required for success in her job. She hired me to help her stay motivated to raise her gross income each month and keep it consistently at that new level. By exploring Joan's old belief system and beginning affirmation work, we were able to accomplish this in a short period of time. After experiencing an initial period of success around increasing and sustaining her sales goals, Joan was now feverishly working to reach a fourth compensation level. That would increase her commissions substantially, but also require her to sell at a consistently higher level each month than she had previously been able to attain.

No matter how hard Joan tried, she continued to fall short of reaching that elusive fourth level. When I suggested there was no doubt in my mind she could bring in an amount higher than she was aiming for, Joan became quite resistant and angry toward me. After some gentle prodding, she recognized her resistance, but she did not know how to stop it, and began to understand that something deeper was going on. As we began to talk about her reaction and what might be causing such fierce resistance, Joan had an epiphany. She realized that she didn't feel comfortable with or worthy of earning the amount of money the fourth compensation level would bring.

Once Joan understood the reasons for her discomfort about earning such a large amount of money, we were able to attack her self-limited thinking and propel her forward. I pushed Joan to move beyond her comfort zone and helped her see that scarcity thinking had made these new numbers unattainable. I explained that by changing her belief system and allowing herself to imagine that she could easily produce this income each month, she would break through the self-created barrier. Joan created a vision and goals that spanned several months, which she supported with affirmations. The result of Joan's work with visioning and affirmations was that she reached her fourth level earning goal within a six-month period.

In learning to let go, we begin to understand that while perhaps initially uncomfortable, change does not restrict us but ultimately gives us new freedom and greater power. Joan's story is a perfect example of how releasing old thought patterns and making changes will improve your life.

3. Visualization Is a Tool That Can Help Us Reprogram Our Thinking

Visions are statements of possibility. They transcribe onto our imagination everything we want and desire. They reflect our true inner voice, not that of someone else. Visualizations, on the other hand, are the mental pictures of our visions — the images of what we desire to manifest. Because we form them and carry them around in our minds, these pictures are always with us.

Imagination is the ability to use our minds to create mental pictures, or an inner sense of feeling/knowing about something that is not present or has never been experienced. It is important to understand that we constantly use our imagination whether we are conscious of it or not. Every time you think about all the potential negative outcomes of a situation, you are using your imagination. Rather than focus on what we don't want, why not use our subconscious mind to achieve the results we do want and deserve?

4. The Leading Achievers Development Wheel

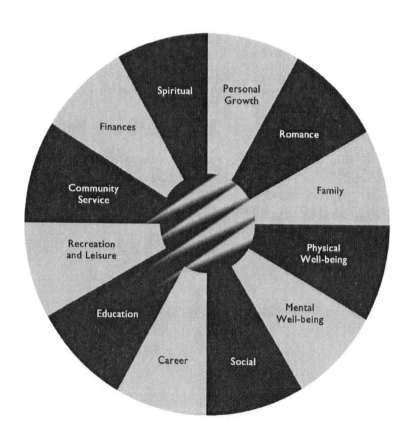

The graphic on page 92 is the Leading Achievers Development Wheel. This tool is going to help you create a new life that *reflects what you want for yourself* using the methods we have already discussed and some new ones. This wheel will help you set in motion powerful forces that will feed into the Law of Attraction and enable you to create the life you truly desire. The wheel is divided into the 12 major life areas. The steps you will use to create a life vision can also be used for your goals around each of the life areas, for an event you would like to have happen, a person you want to meet, or a situation you'd like to create. It doesn't matter how large or how small your desire is.

As you can see, career comprises only one section of the wheel; this is a purposeful observation. It is essential that we realize the truth in that old axiom: All work and no play makes for a dull person. To focus on work at the virtual exclusion of all else also prevents you from benefiting from the energy created through play, good relationships, and giving to others. Anyone who still believes that consistently working 50- to 60-hour weeks is necessary to achieve success is flat-out wrong. A person might be able to continue at that pace for a while, but eventually burnout — or serious illness — will set in, and they will no longer have the energy to be creative or live in possibility.

When we give ourselves permission to have a life beyond work, we free up our energy so that when we do sit down to focus on work, we are more relaxed and able to work faster and with better results. Don't believe it? Try it for a week — you may be surprised by the results.

Other aspects of the vision wheel include personal growth, romance, family, physical well-being, mental well-being, social contact/relationships, career, education, recreation and leisure, community service, finances, and spiritual growth.

5. Skirting the Fear Trap

In her book *Creative Visualization*, Shakti Gawain tells us that
sometimes an individual will have trouble visualizing or imagining
what they desire. Somewhat understandably, fear is typically the
culprit that prevents someone from being able to visualize. At its
root, this fear is likely the anticipated discomfort about
confronting difficult feelings and emotions and working them
through. Gawain goes on to say, "The truth is that there is nothing
within us that can hurt us; it is only our fear of experiencing our
own feelings that can keep us trapped . . ." Remember, once you
allow yourself to look fully and deeply at the source of a fear, its
power over you diminishes.

At this point, you may want to go back and review our
discussion of fear on page 43.

6. Setting the Stage to Create Visions That Work

The most important aspect of the visualization practice is to make it
a habit. For example, whenever I go into a meeting, whether with a
group or with an individual, I always create a vision for what I want
to occur during that meeting using the steps described below.

Before you begin work with the wheel make sure you are
completely relaxed (see the relaxation exercise on p.129) and in
a place where you will not be disturbed. If you are new to this
type of work, you might want to visit almost any bookstore and
invest in a guided meditation CD. Another option that might help
you calm down and relax is to read a spiritual or meditative book.
Perhaps you can take a walk in a park, or simply sit quietly
outside by yourself. Each person will find the technique that
works best for them.

Once you have relaxed and are ready to begin, say the
following affirmation:

**"As I start to think about what I want to be,
I begin to move toward what I can be."**

Once you are willing to use your mind's eye to create visions for every goal you have, you dramatically increase your chances for success. Here are four suggestions for creating visions that work:

1. Passion — You must be totally clear and passionate about what you desire or want to do. A mild yearning will not do — this must be a burning desire. The clearer and more focused you are about the desire, the more quickly your vision will manifest.

2. Belief — You must truly believe you can have and are worthy of your desire. If you're not quite to the point where you can truly believe in your worthiness, it is okay to "act as if" while you are in the process of changing your old habits, attitudes, and beliefs.

3. Positivity — Your intentions must be good, healthy, and positive. Negative intentions may initially bring you what you desire, but the manifestation will invariably be short-lived.

4. Acceptance — Sometimes we have certain talents and discover we are not open to these gifts, or that we actually don't want them. Begin to practice acceptance by "acting as if." Use your imagination to create mental pictures of what you are trying to achieve until you are able to do so without thinking about it.

When you are ready to create a vision, remember to always write it down. Recording your vision in writing is the first step toward manifesting the physical aspect of it. Writing down your vision is essential because at that point in the process you are moving your thoughts from the intangible to the tangible.

A self-assessment process that includes examining "Where am I today?" and comparing that to "Where do I want to be tomorrow?" helps stimulate the imagination to create the strongest visions. Let's look at these two steps more closely.

By assessing where we are today, we are pinpointing the exact problem or area of our life that is not working. This requires going deep within ourselves to honestly face and confront any discomfort with the situation. Only then can we begin to create a picture or idea of what life would look like without the discomfort this problem is causing. So, vision creation involves the process of forming a mental picture of what our life would look like without problems, anxieties, embarrassments, or worries.

You can use this book — or purchase a special journal or bound book in which to write your life visions. Remember, this is the start of the new life you are creating. Since you are worthy of only the best in all things, your vision journal should be no exception. Write a dedication to yourself inside the front cover. You want to take every step possible to show the Universe how special you know you are.

7. Using the Leading Achievers Development Wheel

The first step in creating a vision is taking a self-assessment. When you visit your doctor, he or she asks you to pinpoint the exact areas that are causing you pain or discomfort and to describe the exact nature of the pain. In much the same way, when you desire to make life changes, you must first look inside yourself and pinpoint the exact areas and nature of your pain or discomfort. As you begin to think about the person you want to become, you begin moving toward the person you can become.

Phase I

Before you pick up your pen and start writing, ask yourself the following questions and just think about their answers. Where are you struggling or finding life unmanageable? Where is your life working, or manageable? What is the exact nature of your discomfort? Where does your life feel out of balance? Is it work? Your significant relationship? Your relationship with your family? Your spiritual life? Your health? Your finances? It's okay if you're experiencing difficulty in more than one area — the key is to specifically identify the area(s) where you are struggling.

Now pick up your pen and write in the space provided below, or in your journal, the question, **"Where am I today?"** Then underneath it, write the first heading, **Personal Growth**. Think and then write about what your growth has been like over the past few years — where have you grown and where have you stopped growing? What are you doing and not doing to move yourself forward? Where is your life manageable and where is it unmanageable? What is causing you pain and discomfort each day? Take the time to be as descriptive as possible. Record all of your feelings, and above all, be honest with yourself. When you have finished writing under the first heading, write the next heading, **Romance**, and repeat the process until you have written about all 12 sections of the wheel.

As you write and go through this part of the exercise, think of yourself as visiting the doctor and pinpointing what's not working and what is. Be as descriptive as possible. Identify what, exactly, is causing you pain and discomfort in each of the 12 areas of the wheel. For example, have you been passed over for a promotion at work that you feel should rightfully have been yours? Are you feeling lonely inside your significant relationship? Have you been single for a while and wishing you had a significant relationship? Is it loneliness? Bitterness? Anxiety? Fear? Shame? Guilt? Be as descriptive as possible and honest about your feelings. Use the example below to help you understand the level of detail and emotion you want to describe.

Example – Personal Growth

I started meditating and taking a half-hour for myself each day, but stopped after two months. Now I always seem to have way too much on my plate each day to take even five minutes for myself. The last time I read a good novel was last winter when I took a rare four-day weekend. I bought a great self-help book but resisted doing the exercises. I rarely stop for lunch during my workday, and when I do eat, it's at my desk. I want to plan a "real" vacation this winter but I've had no time to check prices or itineraries online.

My life seems to be getting busier and busier. I always seem to be looking forward to the time I can relax, but it never seems to happen. I am overcommitted, overwhelmed, and completely unsatisfied.

My husband always seems to have time for himself, and I'm beginning to feel very angry about not having time for myself. I'm growing more and more resentful of my spouse and my children. They seem to be increasingly needy, and I'm less patient than I have ever been . . .

Phase I: Where Am I Today?

Personal Growth

_____

_____

_____

_____

_____

_____

_____

_____

_____

_____

_____

Romance

_____

_____

_____

_____

_____

_____

_____

_____

_____

_____

_____

_____

Family

_____

_____

_____

_____

_____

_____

_____

_____

_____

_____

Physical Well-Being

_____

_____

_____

_____

_____

_____

_____

_____

_____

_____

_____

_____

Mental Well-Being

_____

_____

_____

_____

_____

_____

_____

_____

_____

_____

Social Contact/Relationships

_____

_____

_____

_____

_____

_____

_____

_____

_____

_____

_____

_____

Career

_____

_____

_____

_____

_____

_____

_____

_____

_____

_____

Education

_____

_____

_____

_____

_____

_____

_____

_____

_____

_____

_____

Recreation and Leisure

_____

_____

_____

_____

_____

_____

_____

_____

_____

_____

_____

Community Service

_____

_____

_____

_____

_____

_____

_____

_____

_____

_____

_____

_____

Finances

_____

_____

_____

_____

_____

_____

_____

_____

_____

_____

Spiritual Growth

_____

_____

_____

_____

_____

_____

_____

_____

_____

_____

_____

Phase II

After you have completed the first part of the exercise, take a break. You may want to reread it, and perhaps add more to it the next day. When you are ready, begin the second phase. However, do not let too much time elapse between completing the first and second parts of the assessment.

For Phase II, write in the space provided below, or write in your journal, the question "Where do I want to be?" Then underneath it, write the first heading, Personal Growth. Think and then write about what you want from your personal growth in the next year. Now it's time to use your imagination. It is important to write, in present tense, a vision that describes what your life feels like without all the discomfort. It is critical that you imagine your vision as if it already exists, exactly the way you want it to be. Describe yourself in the setting or environment where you want to be, surrounded by the people you will be interacting with, and noticing in detail how you relate to one another. Write, picture, and think as if every detail of this experience is already happening.

Imagine yourself and your life without your existing problems. Describe what it looks like for each heading of the wheel. How do you feel? How do you spend your time? What kinds of books do you read? What kinds of music do you listen to? What kinds of movies do you watch? Do you remain at the same job? Do you keep the same friends and continue existing relationships?

Get detailed about your new life. What does it look like? How does it smell? What does it taste like? What kinds of textures are there in it for you to touch? What kinds of wonderful exotic tastes do you encounter? Remember, this is your preferred future — be as detailed as possible about what your newly manifested life looks like. It's important to remain focused on the results of your manifestations; do not let your intellectual brain be disturbed by thoughts about how it will happen.

Recognize that change is challenging. It is not going to occur overnight, nor is it going to be easy to accept. Change is something you will likely have to grow into. Therefore, **it is absolutely okay to build a vision for yourself that is beyond what you believe is possible at this moment.**

Use your entire imagination — and go for it! Remember to include all the details. Be as specific as possible.

Example

I am leaving work a half-hour earlier and using the time at home for myself. When I get home, I spend time with the children before I make dinner. Dinner has now become a family project, and everyone has an assigned role. Sometimes we have time in the morning to chop and prepare things for that evening's meal. My husband does the dishes and helps the kids with their homework while I take the time to meditate.

We have taught the children to do their own laundry and everyone now chips in, based on a schedule we have set up. I take a yoga class twice a week. One of the classes is on the weekend, and afterward I go for tea with a few of the women I meet in my class. These are women like myself, who are in the process of releasing stress and living more fulfilled lives.

On the weekends, I take time to read my self-help books, including doing the exercises. I now belong to a once-a-month support group, which includes some of the women from my yoga class. We are all growing closer each month, and forming very tight bonds.

At night I stop doing household things by nine o'clock, no matter what. My new mantra is, "Tomorrow is another day." I no longer do work after the children go to bed. Instead, I spend that time reading the newspaper and current novels, or enjoying time with my husband. I have cut down on afterwork meetings and am now involved in only two organizations. We have hired a house helper who comes in every week. Our winter vacation is planned — we have tickets for Disneyland...

Phase II: Where Do I Want to Be?

Personal Growth

_____

_____

_____

_____

_____

_____

_____

_____

_____

_____

_____

_____

_____

Romance

_____
_____
_____
_____
_____
_____
_____
_____
_____
_____
_____

Family

_____
_____
_____
_____
_____
_____
_____
_____
_____
_____
_____

Physical Well-Being

_____

_____

_____

_____

_____

_____

_____

_____

_____

_____

Mental Well-Being

_____

_____

_____

_____

_____

_____

_____

_____

_____

_____

Social Contact/Relationships

_____

_____

_____

_____

_____

_____

_____

_____

_____

_____

_____

Career

_____

_____

_____

_____

_____

_____

_____

_____

_____

_____

_____

Education

_____

_____

_____

_____

_____

_____

_____

_____

_____

_____

_____

Recreation and Leisure

_____

_____

_____

_____

_____

_____

_____

_____

_____

_____

_____

_____

Community Service

_____

_____

_____

_____

_____

_____

_____

_____

_____

_____

_____

Finances

_____

_____

_____

_____

_____

_____

_____

_____

_____

_____

_____

_____

Spiritual Growth

_____

_____

_____

_____

_____

_____

_____

_____

_____

_____

_____

Congratulations! You have now written a vision for your life. In vision creation, the greater the clarity and details, the greater the quality and power of the imprint. After you have written your visions, prioritize what you have written under each heading. Then think about the visions at least once a day. But stay relaxed and try not to put too much pressure on yourself. While concentrating on your vision, stay confident and send it positive energy. Use positive affirmations to assert that your vision has manifested or is manifesting, and then express your gratitude.

8. You've Got to Be Kidding!

Right now, you may be more than a little skeptical, perhaps wondering if it's really possible that this process can work for you. I promise you that it does work! I've seen hundreds of people succeed using this method. It's okay if you're still dubious, as long as you're willing to try it out. Here are 10 tips to help you get started.

1. Create affirmations to support your visions. These are positive thoughts and statements you will repeat over and over to yourself, at least twice a day.

2. Make a collage by cutting out pictures from magazines, catalogues, newspapers, etc. that support your vision. Post it in a location where you will see it regularly. When you look at your collage, envision yourself doing the things represented by the pictures.

3. Read as much as you can on the subjects of positive thinking and the Law of Attraction. The library is full of motivational books — or you can listen to CDs or tapes in your car. Listen to these recordings again and again. *See the bibliography at the end of this book for suggestions.*

4. Create your own personal affirmation tapes or CDs. Record yourself speaking your affirmations with music you find motivating and inspirational in the background. Listen to them repeatedly.

5. Surround yourself with people who also are working on changing themselves and who think positively. This may mean letting go of some of your old, toxic relationships. Think about this example: You remove a sick tree from a forest of sick trees, and give it the TLC it needs to heal. However, if you put that same tree back in the sick

forest once it's gotten healthy, the tree will become sick again and likely will die. Be careful about whom you allow to join your most influential circle.

6. Continually remind yourself that the Law of Attraction is at work in your life. This means that you always have a choice to do things differently. You know the old saying, "Keep on doing what you've always done and you'll keep on getting what you've always gotten." The decision to change — or not — is yours.

7. Learn how to meditate, or spend at least a half-hour each day by yourself in total silence, doing nothing. There are many types of meditation. Meditation — the practice of focusing on the space between your thoughts — requires you to take some time out of your busy life to simply sit and be. In order to make progress on your life goals, you must take some quiet time for yourself every day. While quiet meditation is truly beneficial, if you prefer, taking long walks by yourself or jogging can serve as that alone time. If a half-hour is too difficult to manage at first, begin with five minutes and gradually increase the duration by increments of five minutes.

8. Get in the habit of journaling. Find a blank book you really love and use it to record your thoughts, goals, and desires. You can even use it as a way to understand your fears. Just because you begin this process does not mean the fears and self-sabotage will immediately abate. You still will have doubts — this is normal. Use your journal to answer your own concerns about your fears,

creating a "dialogue" about why the fears are irrational or unlikely to come true. During your alone time, journaling is one of the best ways to figure out what is bothering you.

9. Find a mentor or coach who has done this sort of work and can provide guidance from his or her experience. Look for someone who will truly be there to support you during your transition.

10. Locate a support group where several people meet regularly to work on changing themselves — or form one of your own. Remember, two people count as a group.

Chapter Two
The Power of Affirmations

1. How Affirmations Work

Affirmations are an important part of creating visions. They become the goals of our visions. They also can replace the endless mind chatter that continues to comment about our lives and how we are doing. After you have spent several days thinking about your visions, start to create affirmations that will support them.

Let's examine how affirmations work.

Affirmations are simply statements of our thoughts. Therefore they can be positive or negative. When we consciously use positive affirmations (thoughts), they are a fast, safe method through which we can successfully reprogram old, negative self-talk, and not only set but achieve our goals. Many successful people, including professional athletes, motivational speakers, and movie stars use affirmations to bring their goals and dreams into reality.

The power of affirmations is limited only by an individual's personal conviction and belief that the affirmations are working. If the affirmations are used only done half-heartedly, the results will manifest accordingly. But if a person is focused and believes passionately in achieving the goal stated in their affirmation, then the situation will almost surely manifest optimally.

The magician Merlin, of the timeless Arthurian legends, was fabled to end his affirmations with the powerful phrase *"and so shall it be!"* The power behind his words, offered to the Universe, was unforgettable. Merlin had no doubt in his mind that his words would manifest into his desired outcome. And so they did. Our affirmations can be that powerful, too.

As we begin and continue to practice our affirmations, we will start to see them manifest in our lives. The best way to keep our affirmations handy and organized is to write them on index cards. One way to track the power and success of our affirmations is to keep our old affirmation cards and periodically review them to see how quickly and easily we were able to manifest those changes in our lives. It's important to remember to regularly update our affirmation cards as our situations change and we create new visions.

2. The Art of Detachment

Although we may have a specific outcome in mind for our affirmations, it always helps to remain a little open-minded about how the outcome will manifest. This gives the Universe plenty of leeway to provide for our needs and desires. Once we affirm something by putting our message out into the Universe, we have to allow it the freedom to respond in its own speed, time, and manner. This is a process known as detachment.

We have goals that we think and speak about and write down as affirmations, but once we release them, we must detach from their outcome. The Universe may respond to our affirmations with a completely unexpected result, but in order for that to happen, we must allow from the outset that we are amenable to an alternate outcome, particularly if it serves us more fully than the desire we originally affirmed.

3. Uses for Affirmations

- Access your psychic abilities and intuition
- Allow the free flow of emotions
- Alter bad karma/change your karmic path
- Attract new business/clients/employment/promotions
- Attract wonderful, positive, supportive people into your life
- Clear physical/emotional/spiritual blockages
- Create loving relationships
- Create prosperity and abundance
- Develop your mind
- Discern your life's purpose
- Evolve your body
- Further your personal well-being and health
- Grow spiritually
- Learn forgiveness
- Lose weight
- Love yourself
- Manifest your ideal career
- Receive a soul message

4. Develop Your Own Affirmations

Positive Keywords to Use in Your Affirmations

Abundant	Enthusiasm	Permanent
Acceptance	Expert	Positive
Appreciate	Good	Prosperous
Attract	Happiness	Radiate
Beautiful	Harmonious	Rapport
Bliss	Improve	Security
Brilliant	Intelligent	Sincere
Courage	Love	Support
Delightful	Meaningful	Willingness
Effortlessly	Optimism	Wisdom
Endless	Peace	Wonderful

Lack of internal goal setting is the single biggest factor blocking most people from achieving their true potential. For many individuals, the key to unlocking unlimited success is only an affirmation away. Use the relaxation method on page 129, or an alternate method of your choice. Once you feel deeply relaxed, open your eyes and begin the next exercise.

In longhand, write the following affirmation:

I effortlessly write affirmations and take the time each day to imprint new heights of greatness.

_____

_____

_____

_____

_____

Select a goal from **Uses for Affirmations** (page 119) or one of the goal areas you focused on with the vision wheel. Then choose a specific topic and create your affirmation, one that will serve you in making necessary life changes. Write it below.

_____

_____

_____

_____

_____

_____

Give some thought to which specific keywords have a positive effect on your subconscious. These are words that inspire you, challenge you, comfort you, uplift you. They can be from favorite quotes, readings, posters, bumper stickers, magazines, novels — anyplace, as long as they motivate you to take the necessary steps to move forward. Write them below. See the list of words on page 120 for ideas.

_____

_____

_____

_____

_____

_____

_____

_____

_____

What barriers or negative self-talk do you need to replace with affirmations that will help you improve your outlook and achieve your goals? Write them here. For example, many people repeatedly say they "are sorry" to others even though it is inappropriate for the situation. This is a barrier to exhibiting self-confident behavior. A positive affirmation would be, "I have stopped apologizing for myself to others."

_____

_____

_____

_____

_____

Practice creating two different affirmations around the same goal.

PART 1

Toward your desired end result. Step forward in time and see one of your goals accomplished. Describe the accomplishment in present tense and positive terms. For example, "I now am in a new job with a boss who appreciates my skills and efforts."

_____

_____

_____

_____

_____

_____

_____

PART 2

Eliminating the barrier(s) to your desired end result.
Reread your answer to PART 1 and answer the question, "What would this goal look like if I could magically erase the barriers to accomplishing it?" For example, "I am succeeding in my new job while being supported by my network of friends and associates. My manager is complimentary of my skills and encourages me to try new things."

_____

_____

_____

_____

_____

_____

_____

_____

_____

_____

Select one of the two affirmations from the previous exercise and rewrite it, using words from your personal list of keywords on page 121.

_____

_____

_____

_____

_____

5. Creating Effective Affirmations

Follow these guidelines to create the most powerful affirmations possible.

1. **Make your affirmations personal.** It is only possible to affirm for yourself. When you write your affirmations, include the words "I" or "I am."

2. **Use positive imagery in your affirmations.** Many of us work best when we can see (visualize) the affirmation's outcome. To that end, your affirmations must trigger positive mental pictures. For example, affirm "I have a slim, healthy body," as opposed to "I am no longer overweight."

3. **Be specific in your affirmations.** We sometimes have a tendency to generalize our goals with broad strokes. The more specific you can be in the language of your affirmations the better. Do you aspire to become a famous writer? What do you want to write — novels, a gritty exposé, a cookbook, magazine articles, screenplays, poetry, sales copy, greeting cards, pop songs? How famous do you want to be? A celebrity in your own town? A *New York Times* best selling author? A household name? Be as specific as possible with each affirmation.

4. **Form your affirmations in the present tense.** It is more effective to affirm "I am Seattle's most successful portrait photographer" versus "I will be Seattle's most successful portrait photographer."

5. **Indicate achievement in your affirmations.** You may not have the skills yet, but you do already possess the ability to do whatever you want to accomplish. To that end, affirming "I can" will not empower your outcome. Instead, use language like "I do," "I am," etc.

6. **Avoid comparisons in your affirmations.** Individuals with high self-esteem have no need to compare themselves to others. Set specific, personal goals for yourself. Do not worry about what others are doing or how successful they are. To compare yourself to someone else is to invite inevitable feelings of inferiority. Be who you are, with honesty and integrity, and don't worry about anyone else.

7. **Use action and emotion words in your affirmations.** Use strong action words and vibrant emotion words to affirm your accomplishments.

   Examples include:
   "I easily attain . . ."
   "I joyfully achieve . . ."
   "I lovingly relate . . ."
   "I enthusiastically claim . . ."
   "I energetically pursue . . ."

8. **Be accurate and realistic in your affirmations.** Affirm only as far as you can honestly see yourself. Be positive about who you are, your talents and abilities, and your potential — but be realistic. If you are 5 feet 5 inches tall, it would be unrealistic to create an affirmation that you are a 6-foot-7-inch NBA forward.

Affirm possibilities, not perfection. Avoid such phrases as "I always" or "I never."

9. **Strive for balance in your affirmations.** Create affirmations around all areas of your life, not just in the ones that occupy most of your attention right now.

R$_x$ercise

Make a list of your current goals and apply the above steps, creating one to three affirmations around each goal. This is also a perfect place to create goals (affirmations) for your Life Vision.

_____

_____

_____

_____

_____

_____

_____

_____

_____

_____

_____

_____

_____

_____

After writing your new affirmations, simply review the checklist and ask yourself if the affirmation satisfies each of the following requirements:

[ ] It is personal.

[ ] It is positive.

[ ] It is specific.

[ ] It is present tense.

[ ] It indicates achievement.

[ ] It does not make comparisons.

[ ] It uses strong action words and vibrant emotion words.

[ ] It is accurate and realistic.

[ ] It contributes to balance in my life.

If the affirmation does not meet all of these requirements, tweak it and make the necessary adjustments. Through repeated application, this checklist will become second nature to you, and your affirmation process will be simple and effortless.

⇨Create at least two affirmations for each one of the visions you wrote for the 12 sections of the development wheel. Categorize them according to the goal or life categories to which they pertain, or the sections of the Leading Achiever Development Wheel. Write them on index cards so you can easily access and read them each day.

⇨As you imprint each affirmation, first visualize the goal on which it is based to add meaning and purpose. Be as clear as possible in creating the picture of you achieving that goal. Cut out magazine pictures that represent images of your goals and paste them next to your affirmations.

The imprinting process involves three steps:

1. Read the affirmation out loud.

2. Vividly picture the experience/event/end result as if it were happening right now.

3. Feel the emotion related to your accomplishment.

Review your affirmations at least twice a day, in a relaxed state of mind. It is preferable to do it when you first awaken in the morning and before you go to bed at night.

6. Steps for Maximizing the Effectiveness of Your Affirmations

⇨ Work with your affirmations at the same time each day — morning is good, but find the time that works best for you.

⇨ Relax and meditate for just a few minutes before you think/speak/write your affirmations to connect with your intuitive higher self.

⇨ Think/speak/write your affirmations clearly and slowly.

⇨ Affirm with meaning and feeling.

⇨ Feel the power behind your thoughts, words, and declarations.

⇨Relax for a moment or so afterwards to complete the integration of the affirmations.

⇨Keep your affirmations to yourself. Confidentiality supports the constructive nature of your affirmations. Be judicious about to whom you reveal them. Share them only with those who need to know and who will support you.

7. Relaxation Exercise
For Use before Beginning Your Imprinting Process

Say the following words to yourself and imagine doing the relaxing actions described below:

I relax my head, I relax my scalp, I relax my forehead, I relax my jaw. I relax my neck, I relax my throat, I relax my tongue, I relax my shoulders, I relax my chest, I relax my upper back, I relax my lower back. I relax my arms, I relax my abdomen, I relax my legs. My breathing is peaceful, slow, and steady.

Now say to yourself out loud:

I am willing to let go. I release, I let go. I release all tension. I release all fear. I release all anger. I release all guilt. I release all sadness. I let go of all my old limitations. I let go and I am at peace. I am at peace with myself. I am at peace with the process of life. I am at peace with the world around me. I am safe.

8. Sample Affirmations

The affirmations listed below will help you get started. You can begin with these and eventually change them to fit your personal situations and needs.

Love Yourself

I am very special. I like who I am, and I feel good about myself.

I continually improve myself and I am growing every day. I like who I am today.

I would rather be me than anyone else in the world.

I respect myself and approve of who I am.

I approve of myself in all situations and I approve of who I am.

I have many wonderful qualities. I recognize and honor my talents, skills, and abilities as unique to me.

I am positive and confident. I consistently radiate out and attract much good to me.

I am a valuable and important person, and worthy of respect from others at all times.

I am kind, compassionate, and gentle with myself.

I am a beautiful person inside and out.

I like who I am, and I'm glad to be me.

Evolve Your Body

I am unique . . . from the top of my head to the bottom of my feet. I love and accept my body.

I am at home in my body.

I lovingly care for my body.

I am good to my body and my body is good to me.

I nourish my body with good thoughts and healthy food.

I recognize my body as a good friend.

I choose to create peace in my mind, body, and world.

Clear Physical/Emotional/Spiritual Blockages

I love life and am grateful to be alive.

I am a special person with many gifts.

I have lots of energy, enthusiasm, and vitality. I am excited to be me.

I use kind, loving words. I am free of negative emotions.

I smile a lot; I am happy on the inside and outside.

I am warm, sincere, honest, and genuine.

Develop Your Mind

I have a quick and alert mind. I am intelligent and know the right thing to say.

My mind is cleansed and free. I leave the past and move into the new.

My higher self is now operating in my mind, body, and affairs, whether I see it or not.

I have a wonderful sense of humor and exercise it easily.

I have all the divine activities and ideas I need. I move forward right now.

I am a decisive person. I follow through and support myself with love.

Allow the Free Flow of Emotions

I consistently feel confident, self-assured, and self-reliant.

I accept and give compliments easily.

I am a kind, lovable person. I radiate love to everyone I meet.

I have great joy for being alive. I enjoy everything I do. I feel happy and blissful just being alive.

I am in such control of my emotions that nothing can disturb my peace of mind.

Grow Spiritually

I am safe and secure and guided.

Divine love works through me and for me.

Divine love dissolves all obstacles and clears the way for my success.

My faith is built upon a rock and my heart's desire now comes to pass, under grace in a miraculous way.

I water my wilderness with faith and suddenly it blossoms as the rose.

I appreciate all the blessings I have.

I watch my words, thoughts, and actions because they are all-powerful and will bring their effect into my life.

Attract Wonderful, Positive, Supportive People into Your Life

I love everyone and everyone loves me. I turn enemies into friends and cement my chain of good.

*I am at peace with myself and the whole world.
I am fully and completely at ease with other people, at all times and in all situations.*

I set a great example for others.

I am warm and friendly toward all people. I treat everyone equally, with consideration and respect.

Further Your Health and Well-Being

I am relaxed and centered. I have plenty of time to get things done.

I nourish my body with healthy food.

I enjoy everything I do.

I am vibrantly healthy and radiantly beautiful.

I am always safe and divinely protected and guided.

I choose to be healthy and free.

I breathe freely and fully. I am safe. I trust the process of life.

Create Loving Relationships

*My relationship with _____
grows more joyful and fulfilling each day.*

I attract only loving relationships in my life; all others slip away.

As I nurture myself, those around me are nurtured.

I feel tolerance and compassion for all those I love, myself included.

I'm valuable and special just as I am. I let go of all relationships that determine my value.

Create Prosperity and Abundance

I am worthy and deserve the best life has to offer.

I trust there is plenty for all as this is an abundant Universe.

I am enough; I do enough; I have enough.

Abundance is my natural state of being.

I grow more financially prosperous each day.

The more I have, the more I have to give.

It is okay for me to have all I want.

I have everything I need to enjoy my life here and now.

The Universe is the unfailing, unlimited source of all my supply.

I accept all the joy and prosperity life has to offer me.

Discern Your Life's Purpose

I live in the present. I eagerly welcome and examine each moment as it arrives.

I recognize, accept, and follow the divine plan of my life.

I accept my divine plan as it is revealed to me step by step.

There is only one plan, the Universe's plan, and that plan now comes to pass.

I let go of everything not divinely designed for me, and the perfect plan of my life now comes to pass.

Attract New Business/Clients/Employment/Promotions

I am interested in many things, and my skills and talents are always needed.

I have the perfect job, boss, and peers.

I am totally open and receptive to a wonderful new position, one that uses all my talents and abilities and allows me to express creativity.

I offer services that are always in demand and can pick and choose what to do.

I earn good money while doing work that satisfies me.

I am always in my right place, doing my right work, at the right time, for the right pay.

I am my own expert and I allow others the same privilege.

I continually find ways to motivate myself and others.

Forgiveness

I forgive everyone and everyone forgives me.

I am free from mistakes and the consequences of mistakes.
I forgive _____ for _____ and let them go free.

I forgive myself for _____ and let myself go free.

Time Management

I am an action-oriented person; I accomplish goals, one thing at a time.

It's fun and easy being organized.

I am alert to and welcome opportunities as they present themselves.

I plan my time effectively. I plan my work and work my plan.

Miscellaneous

Everything comes to me easily and effortlessly.

I communicate clearly and effectively.

I am always in the right place at the right time, successfully engaging in the right activity.

I am the master of my life. Everything I need is already within me.

I am happy and successful.

I recognize my worth and feel wonderful about myself.

Conclusion

We are here to learn and grow. We are love, and our entire life is geared toward learning to love ourselves. When we can see the love that is in us, we can see this light in others. Then we will prosper personally and help the world to change as well. Every person who heals themselves automatically helps hundreds of people around them to heal.

Today I understand the relentless need my parents had for me to be perfect so they could feel perfect. It was a great gift to me in many ways. Their need manifested in me a drive and determination to discover who I really am, and find the peace and wholeness of my being.

My parents made their own sacrifice. Neither one of them was able to let go of their fear long enough to feel their own inner peace. My dad's devotion to his religion left an indelible mark on me. I know that he introduced me — through his ritual and prayers — to the understanding that there was something very special about me. He led me to see the sacredness that exists in all of us, and the ability we all have to develop a relationship with a Power that is greater than ourselves and only wants what's good for us.

By forming a relationship with my higher self, I developed the freedom to not only forgive my parents but myself. Forgiveness has been the ultimate act of healing on my journey. As I learned to accept the reasons I was so unhappy, and my initial need to demean myself, I was able to forgive myself for not knowing any other way to handle my thinking and actions up to that point in my life. Forgiving myself cleared my mind, and I was able to forgive those around me. The prize was great freedom. No longer do I view myself as a victim of others. Instead, I can understand and clearly see the pain they are experiencing.

Two of the hardest parts of my journey have been the ability to recognize my feelings and then express them to others in an appropriate way, so that I did not suppress or implode them. Learning to express my needs and desires without anger or passive-aggressive behavior took much trial and error. The fear of the repercussions from telling someone I am hurt by their actions, and then informing them of what I need instead, can still scare me silly. Yet I know that taking these steps has led me to a path of personal empowerment and true intimacy with the people in my life.

By practicing repeatedly with the tools in this book, today I can automatically pull myself out of despair, and feelings of shame or low self-worth, in seconds. My perseverance in doing everything I was inspired to do — to help me change — has paid off in more ways than I can describe.

Since you have finished reading this book, I now ask you to go back and complete the exercises. While you are doing this, search out the people in your life who will support you in making the changes you desire. Find new ways of meditating, use affirmations daily, write your life vision, journal, go to lectures, listen to CDs on all areas of this subject, and explore the different types of groups that are on the same journey. If initially you have trouble finding the right people to support you, I strongly suggest you find a coach or therapist. He or she will be able to encourage you and cheer you on, until you can do this for yourself or have found a group of people to support you.

If you are saying to yourself, "I will try to do these things," you are already giving in to your resistance. It's not about trying; it's about doing. It's about commitment — and it is no different than solving a puzzle. To fully experience life involves taking risks and actions that allow you to make mistakes, pick yourself up, and experiment with new behavior until it works. Remember my experience in learning to ride a bike? This journey you are choosing is no different. I know you can do it — so go for it and create the life you've always wanted!

I am asking you to do nothing more that what I did myself. This is how I stayed focused and succeeded. I know you will see some immediate results, but when you begin to feel lost, pull out this book and read my story. Remind yourself that this will be the hardest work you have ever done, yet it will also be the most rewarding.

Bibliography

What follows is a list of books that I have used since the very beginning of my journey. My suggestion is you read *every* book these authors have written and listen to any CD's they have recorded. In addition, periodically go to the bookstore or library and walk up and down the aisles of the self-help section. Allow yourself to let go and you will be led to the books and authors you are supposed to be connecting with in that moment.

You Can Heal Your Life
Louise L.Hay

Think and Grow Rich
Napoleon Hill

Codependent No More: How to Stop Controlling Others and Start Caring for Yourself
Melody Beattie

Secrets of Attraction: The Universal Laws of Love, Sex, and Romance
Sandra Anne Taylor

As a Man Thinketh
James Allen

The Language of Letting Go: Daily Meditations for Codependents
Melody Beattie

Facing Codependence: What it is, Where it Comes From, How it Sabotages Our Lives
Pia Melody

The Wisdom of Florence Scovel Shinn
Florence Scovel Shinn

The Power of Intention: Learning to Co-create Your World Your Way
Dr. Wayne W. Dyer

Creative Visualization: Use the Power of Your Imagination To Create What You Want In Your Life
Shakti Gawain

Power Vs. Force
David R. Hawkins, M.D. Ph.D.

What You Think of Me Is None of My Business
Terry Cole-Whittaker

About the Author

Arlene Rosenberg is a noted international empowerment coach and sought after speaker on awakening and unleashing your potential. She has worked with Citicorp Group, New York Life, Coldwell Banker and Computer Associates, among others. A former corporate executive, she has been called upon to address groups such as the National Association of Women Business Owners (NAWBO), the Alliance of Technology Women (ATW), the New York Society of Security Analysts, and the Arizona Women's Leadership Forum. Through her catalytic approach, participants are taught self-empowerment by learning how to let go of self-limiting behaviors, reprogram their thinking, attract clients, and achieve greater success in their professional and personal lives.

To learn more about Arlene Rosenberg, please visit:

www.therosenberggroup.com

or write to:

The Rosenberg Group Inc.
11778 E. Mariposa Grande Drive
Scottsdale, AZ 85255

Books by

BookMarketingSolutions,LLC
The Publisher of Experts

are available at:

www.ReadingUp.com

This book is available in quantity discounts.

For more information:

info@bookmarketingsolutions.com

or

231.929.1999